After Terror

After Terror:
Promoting Dialogue among Civilizations

Edited by
Akbar Ahmed and Brian Forst

polity

To our grandchildren:
Graham, Ibrahim, Mina, and Samuel,
with love

Contents

Acknowledgments

The editors wish to thank several people who contributed to this book. First, our students, who are the primary reason for our coming together in the first place to engage on such matters. In particular, the enthusiasm and commitment of David Dore, Lenora Fisher, Vassia Gueorguieva, Adam Lankford, and Matthew Powell to the project confirmed our confidence in the judgment and spirit of today's student, especially in working to put the principles of dialogue on the ground in the Washington, DC, area. Our colleagues at American University and our deans, Louis Goodman, Dean of the School of International Service, and William M. LeoGrande, Dean of the School of Public Affairs, were supportive and generous in offering helpful suggestions along the way, as were Dean of Academic Affairs Ivy Broder and Provost Neil Kerwin for their support for the development of a conference to promote the ideas presented in these essays. President Benjamin Ladner's global vision for American University created an especially receptive atmosphere for this project.

We wish also to thank our publisher, Polity Press, and especially Louise Knight for appreciating the concept and shepherding it through the initial editorial process, Andrea Drugan and Sarah Dancy for helping to manage the processes that followed, and Jean van Altena for editing the manuscript in a thoroughly professional and thoughtful manner.

Our greatest debt of gratitude is to the contributing essayists. In making commitments to support and own a vision for a more vibrant future and then making good on them, they wrote this book. It was reassuring to receive this support for the enterprise from such extraordinary people, fascinating to see how each essayist responded to the challenge, and exhilarating to absorb the breadth of their contributions.

Last, not least, we are deeply in the debt of our wives, Judith Forst and Zeenat Ahmed, who have once more indulged us in a project of yet again utmost urgency. Our appreciation for their unwavering support, love, and patience cannot be adequately expressed or sufficiently compensated. They made possible the birth and nurturance of our children and, in turn, their children, to whom we dedicate this book – and to grandchildren every-where. We hope and intend that they will have the good judg-ment to steward humankind in a better direction than has our generation.

Contributor Biographies in Brief

Akbar Ahmed is the Ibn Khaldun Chair of Islamic Studies and Professor of International Relations at American University, Washington, DC. He is former high commissioner (ambassador) of Pakistan to the United Kingdom (1999–2000), a distinguished anthropologist, filmmaker, and the author of numerous articles and books on contemporary Islam, including *Islam under Siege* (Polity, 2003) and *Discovering Islam: Making Sense of Muslim History and Society* (Routledge, 1988), which was the basis of the BBC six-part TV series, "Living Islam." His *Postmodernism and Islam: Predicament and Promise* (Routledge, 1992) was nominated for the Amalfi Award, and his book *Islam Today: A Short Introduction to the Muslim World* (I. B. Tauris, 1999) was awarded best nonfiction book of the year by the *Los Angeles Times*, and his "Jinnah Quartet," a four-part project on Pakistan's founding father, M. A. Jinnah, has won numerous international awards. He has been actively involved in interfaith dialogue and the study of global Islam and its impact on contemporary society. Dr Ahmed has co-edited several books, including *The Future of Anthropology: Its Relevance to the Contemporary World* (Athlone, 1995). Prior to coming to American University, Dr Ahmed was visiting professor and Stewart Fellow in Humanities at Princeton University and held appointments at the Institute for Advanced Study at Princeton, Harvard University, and Cambridge University, where for five years he was the Iqbal Fellow. He is the recipient of the Star of Excellence in Pakistan and the Sir Percy Sykes Memorial Medal given by the Royal Society of Asian Affairs in London. He was recently appointed Trustee of the World Faiths Development

Dialogue by the Archbishop of Canterbury and received the 2002 Free Speech Award from the Muslim Public Affairs Council in Washington, DC. He received the PhD degree in anthropology from the University of London. He was named 2004 District of Columbia Professor of the Year by the Carnegie Foundation for the Advancement of Teaching and the Council for Advancement and Support of Education.

Kofi Annan is Secretary-General of the United Nations, the first to be elected from the ranks of United Nations staff, in 1997. Since joining the UN in 1962, Mr Annan has worked to revitalize the UN through a comprehensive program of reform: to strengthen the UN's traditional work in the development and maintenance of international peace and security, to encourage and advocate human rights, the rule of law, and the universal values of equality, tolerance, and human dignity found in the United Nations Charter, and to restore public confidence in the UN by reaching out to new partners and, in his words, by "bringing the United Nations closer to the people." He was awarded the Nobel Peace Prize in 2001. In conferring the Prize, the Nobel Committee said that Mr Annan "had been pre-eminent in bringing new life to the Organization."

Benjamin R. Barber is the Gershon and Carol Kekst Professor of Civil Society at the University of Maryland and a principal of the Democracy Collaborative, with offices in New York, Washington, and the University of Maryland. A distinguished, internationally renowned political theorist, Dr Barber brings an abiding concern for democracy and citizenship to issues of politics, culture, and education in America and abroad. Professor Barber's 17 books include the classic *Strong Democracy* (University of California Press, 1984) and the best-seller *Jihad vs. McWorld* (originally published by Ballantine in 1995, with a post-9/11 edition in 2001, translated into 20 languages). Professor Barber is a recipient of the Palmes Academiques (Chevalier) from the French Government (2001), the Berlin Prize of the American Academy of Berlin (2001), and the John Dewey Award (2003). He writes frequently for *Harper's*, *The New York Times*, *The Atlantic*, and *The Nation*. He holds a certificate from the London School of Economics and Political Science and MA and Doctorate degrees from Harvard University.

Zbigniew Brzezinski is an internationally recognized authority on global security. He was President Carter's National Security advisor, has taught at Harvard and Columbia universities, and is now a faculty member of The Johns Hopkins University's Nitze School of Advanced International Studies in Washington, DC. Born in Poland in 1928, Dr Brzezinski is the son of a Polish diplomat, spending much of his youth in Canada, France, and Germany. He received a PhD from Harvard in 1953 and became a US citizen in 1958. He was a director of the Trilateral Commission and officer of the Center for Strategic and International Studies. Dr Brzezinski is author of several books on global security and strategy, including *Power and Principle: Memoirs of the National Security Adviser, 1977–1981* (Giroux, 1983) and *Grand Failure: The Birth and Death of Communism in the Twentieth Century* (Collier Books, 1990). His essay in this volume derives largely from his most recent book, *The Choice: Global Domination or Global Leadership* (Basic Books, 2004).

Lord George Carey was the Archbishop of Canterbury from 1991 until 2003, a position to which he rose from humble working-class origins. As Archbishop he established an extraordinary record as independent thinker and activist – for his courageous support for the ordination of women, which received a chilly response from many quarters, for his support of military intervention in Afghanistan, and for his unprecedented efforts to promote interfaith dialogue worldwide. He was the first prominent Western figure to visit Rwanda, in the wake of the genocide in 1995. He subsequently visited Sudan, Mozambique, Egypt, and other spots in the interest of cross-cultural and interfaith dialogue. He is author or editor of several books, including *Freedom and Virtue: The Conservative/Liberation Debate* (ISI Books, 2004), *The Bible for Everyday Life* (Wm B. Eerdmans, 1996), *The Cruelty of Heresy: An Affirmation of Christian Orthodoxy* (SPCK, 1994), *The Church* *in the Marketplace* (Morehouse, 1991), and *The Zodiac and the Salts of Salvation* (Kessenger, 2003).

Diana L. Eck is Professor of Comparative Religion and Indian Studies at Harvard University. She is a member of the Department of Sanskrit and Indian Studies as well as the Faculty of Divinity. In 1996, Professor Eck was appointed to a US State Department Advisory Committee on Religious Freedom Abroad, a 20-member commission that advises the Secretary of State on enhancing and protecting religious freedom and human rights. Her book *Encountering God: A Spiritual Journey from Bozeman to Banaras* (Beacon Press, 1993), a comparative study of religion and religious diversity, won the 1994 Melcher Book Award and the 1995 Louisville Grawemeyer Book Award in Religion. Professor Eck's books on India include *Banaras, City of Light* (Knopf, 1982) and *Darsan: Seeing the Divine Image in India* (Columbia University Press, 1996). In 1998, she received the National Humanities Medal and the National Endowment for the Humanities for her work on American religious pluralism. She received her BA from Smith College (1967) in Religion, her MA from the School of Oriental and African Studies, University of London (1968), in South Asian History, and her PhD from Harvard University (1976) in the Comparative Study of Religion.

Jean Bethke Elshtain is the Laura Spelman Rockefeller Professor of Social and Political Ethics at the University of Chicago, a position to which she was appointed in 1995. She has been a visiting professor at Oberlin College, Yale University, and Harvard University. She is recipient of seven honorary degrees and was elected Fellow of the American Academy of Arts and Sciences in 1996. She is author of *Just War against Terror: The Burden of American Power in a Violent World* (Basic Books, 2003), *Jane Addams and the Dream of American Democracy* (Basic Books, 2002), *Who Are We? Critical Reflections and Hopeful Possibilities* (Wm B. Eerdmans, 2000), *Augustine and the Limits of Politics* (University of Notre Dame Press, 1998), *Democracy on Trial* (Basic Books, 1996), *Women and War* (University of

Chicago Press, 1995), *Meditations on Modern Political Thought* (Praeger, 1986), and *Public Man, Private Woman: Women in Social and Political Thought* (Princeton University Press, 1993). Professor Elshtain has also authored over 400 articles and essays in scholarly journals and journals of civic opinion. She has been a Fellow at the Institute for Advanced Study, Princeton; a Scholar in Residence, Rockefeller Foundation Bellagio Conference and Study Center, Como, Italy; and a Guggenheim Fellow (1991–2).

Amitai Etzioni is an internationally known scholar and a prolific author of books and articles on a vast array of social policy issues. Dr Etzioni was Professor of Sociology at Columbia University for 20 years, after receiving his PhD in Sociology from the University of California in 1958. He was Senior Advisor to the White House on domestic affairs in 1979–80. In 1980, Dr Etzioni was named the first University Professor at The George Washington University, where he directs the Institute for Communitarian Policy Studies. From 1987 to 1989, he served as the Thomas Henry Carroll Ford Foundation Professor at the Harvard Business School. In 1989–90 Dr Etzioni served as founding president of the international Society for the Advancement of Socio-Economics. In 1990, he founded the Communitarian Network, a nonprofit, non-partisan organization dedicated to shoring up society's moral and political foundations. He is editor of *The Responsive Community*, the organization's quarterly journal. Dr Etzioni is the author of 22 books, including *The Monochrome Society* (Princeton University Press, 2001), *The New Golden Rule* (Basic Books, 1996), *The Spirit of Community* (Crown Books, 1993), *The Moral Dimension* (Free Press, 1988), and *From Empire to Community* (Palgrave, 2004).

Brian Forst is Professor of Justice, Law, and Society at the School of Public Affairs, American University, in Washington, DC. Following a distinguished 20-year career in nonprofit research, including service as research director at the Institute for Law and Social Research (1977–85) and the Police Foundation (1985–9), he joined the faculty of The George Washington University in 1989, and then the American University faculty in 1992. He is author of several books, including *Errors of Justice: Nature, Sources and Remedies* (Cambridge University Press, 2004), *The Privatization of Policing: Two Views* (Georgetown University Press, 1999) with Peter Manning, and *Power in Numbers* (Wiley & Sons, 1987), as well as numerous articles, book chapters, and essays on public policy. He chairs the Department of Justice, Law, and Society's doctoral program, serves on the Faculty Senate, and has played cello with the University Orchestra. He was awarded the School of Public Affairs Bernard H. Ross Teaching Excellence Award in 2002. Dr Forst received BS and MBA degrees from The University of California at Los Angeles and a PhD from The George Washington University.

Rajmohan Gandhi is Visiting Professor of Political Science and Director of the Global Crossroads program at the University of Illinois at Urbana/Champaign. Grandson of Mohandas Gandhi, he is an internationally known human rights activist and jury member of the Nuremberg Human Rights Award; a member of the International Council, Initiatives of Change; co-chair of Centre for Dialogue & Reconciliation in Gurgaon, India; and a commentator in *The Hindu* and *The Hindustan Times*. He is renowned for his efforts to promote peace between Hindus and Muslims in his home country, where he has also served as a member of the Rajya. He has authored several books, including *The Good Boatman: A Portrait of Gandhi* (South Asia Books, 2000), and holds BA and MA degrees in economics from St Stephen's College in New Delhi, India.

Walter Isaacson is President of the Aspen Institute, former President and Chief Executive Officer of the CNN News Group, and Managing Editor of *Time Magazine*. He is also a widely published author. Mr Isaacson achieved prominence through his journalism and went on to further acclaim as a leading biographer, in his books on such figures as Benjamin Franklin, Henry Kissinger, Dean Acheson, Averill Harriman, and George F. Kennan. His most recent book, *Benjamin Franklin: An American Life* (Simon and Schuster, 2003), has received much critical acclaim and became a best-seller on all major book review lists.

President Hojjatoleslam Seyed Mohammed Khatami is the fifth president of the Islamic Republic of Iran. Born in 1943 in Ardakan, son of the respected Ayatollah Ruhollah Khatami, President Khatami attended Qom Theology School in 1961, then earned his BA in philosophy from Isfahan University. He entered the University of Tehran in 1970, graduated with an MA, and then returned to Qom to resume his philosophical studies at Qom Seminary. President Khatami represented Ardakan and Meibod constituencies in the first term of Majlis (Parliament) in 1980, and was appointed head of Kayhan newspaper institute by late Ayatollah Khomeini in 1981. In 1992 he was appointed cultural advisor to President Rafsanjani and head of Iran's National Library. In 1996 he was appointed member of the High Council for Cultural Revolution, which he now heads as President. He has written several books and articles on social and cultural issues. In 1998, President Khatami appeared before the United Nations to propose that the UN designate the year 2001 as the Year of Dialogue among Civilizations, with the expressed hope that such a dialogue would contribute to the realization of justice and liberty throughout the world.

Bernard Lewis is Cleveland E. Dodge Professor of Near Eastern Studies, Emeritus, at Princeton University. He is widely regarded throughout the West as the preeminent "Orientalist" scholar, the world's leading authority on the history and culture of Islam. He taught at the University of London until 1974, and afterward until 1986 at Princeton. His books include *The Arabs in History* (Harper Collins, 1950), *The Emergence of Modern Turkey* (Oxford University Press, 1961), *The Assassins* (Basic Books, 2002), *The Muslim Discovery of Europe* (W. W. Norton, 1985), *The Political Language of Islam* (University of Chicago Press, 1988), *Race and Slavery in the Middle East: An Historical Enquiry* (Oxford University Press, 1992), *Islam and the West* (Oxford University Press, 1993), *Islam in History* (Open Court Publishing, 2001), *The Shaping of the*

Modern Middle East (Oxford University Press, 1994), *Cultures in Conflict* (Oxford University Press, 1996), *The Middle East: A Brief History of the Last 2,000 Years* (Scribner, 1995), *The Future of the Middle East* (Orion, 1999), *The Multiple Identities of the Middle East* (Schocken, 2001), *A Middle East Mosaic: Fragments of Life, Letters and History* (Random House, 2000), *What Went Wrong?* (Perennial, 2003), and *The Crisis of Islam: Holy War and Unholy Terror* (Modern Library, 2003). His essays in *The New Yorker, The Atlantic,* and in scholarly journals have been widely read and discussed in recent years, and are considered required reading for Westerners interested in understanding the "clash of civilizations," a phrase he coined in a famous essay in *The Atlantic* in 1990, "The Roots of Muslim Rage."

Martin Marty is Fairfax M. Cone Distinguished Service Professor Emeritus at the University of Chicago, where he taught for 35 years, and George B. Caldwell senior scholar at the Park Ridge Center for the Study of Health, Faith, and Ethics. Professor Marty is author of more than 50 books, including the three-volume *Modern American Religion* (University of Chicago Press, 1997); *The One and the Many: America's Search for the Common Good* (Harvard University Press, 1998); *Education, Religion and the Common Good* (Jossey-Bass, 2000); *Politics, Religion and the Common Good* (Jossey-Bass, 2000); and with photographer Micah Marty, *Places along the Way; Our Hope for Years to Come* (Augsburg Fortress Publisher, 1994) and *When True Simplicity Is Gained* (Wm B. Eerdmans, 1998). His *Righteous Empire* (Harper Collins, 1977) won the National Book Award. His *Martin Luther* (Lipper, 2004) is part of the Penguin Lives series. Past President of the American Academy of Religion and recipient of numerous awards, including the National Humanities Medal and the Medal of the American Academy of Arts and Sciences, Professor Marty has served on two Presidential commissions.

Her Majesty Queen Noor of Jordan was born Lisa Najeeb Halaby in 1951 to a distinguished Arab-American family. She attended schools in Los Angeles, Washington, DC, New York, and Massachusetts, before entering Princeton University in its first co-educational freshman class. After receiving a BA in Architecture and Urban Planning from Princeton in 1974, Queen Noor participated in several international urban planning and design projects in Australia, Iran, the United States, and Jordan. In 1978 she married the late King Hussein of Jordan. Queen Noor has played a significant mediating role and promoted international exchange and understanding of Middle Eastern politics, Arab–Western relations, and current global issues at world affairs organizations, international conferences, and academic institutions. In 1985 Queen Noor established the Noor Al Hussein Foundation (NHF), which initiates and supports national, regional, and international projects in the fields of integrated community development, education, culture, children's welfare, family health, women, and enterprise development.

Joseph S. Nye Jr is Don K. Price Professor of Public Policy and former dean of the Kennedy School at Harvard University. He joined the Harvard faculty in 1964, serving as Director of the Center for International Affairs and Associate Dean of Arts and Sciences. From 1977 to 1979, he was Deputy Undersecretary of State for Security Assistance, Science, and Technology and chaired the National Security Council Group on Nonproliferation of Nuclear Weapons. He returned to Harvard in December of 1995 after serving as Assistant Secretary of Defense for International Security Affairs and Chair of the National Intelligence Council. His most recent books are *Soft Power: The Means to Success in World Politics* (Public Affairs, 2004), *The Paradox of American Power* (Oxford University Press, 2002), and *Understanding International Conflicts*, fourth edition (Longman, 1999); *Power and Interdependence* (Longman, 2000), the third edition of his classic study co-written with Robert O. Keohane; and an edited volume, *For the People: Can We Fix Public Service?* (Brookings, 2003). Professor Nye received his bachelor's degree from Princeton University, did postgraduate work at Oxford University on a Rhodes Scholarship, and earned a PhD in political science from Harvard. A Fellow of the American Academy of Arts and Sciences and of the Academy of Diplomacy, Professor Nye has also been a Senior Fellow of the Aspen Institute and Director of the Aspen Strategy Group.

Judea Pearl is Professor of Artificial Intelligence at the University of California at Los Angeles, since 1970. Award-winning author of numerous books and articles on the representation of reasoning, he is renowned internationally for his pioneering research on probabilistic thinking, inferences about causal mechanisms, learning strategies, and alternative systems of logic. He is today known more widely as father of Daniel Pearl, a reporter for the *Wall Street Journal* until his tragic killing at the hands of terrorists in 2002 in Pakistan. Professor Pearl has distinguished himself by choosing to honor the memory of his son by committing himself to dialogue and cross-cultural understanding in the wake of the tragedy, including a series of dialogues with Akbar Ahmed. "Hatred took the life of my son and hatred I will fight till the end of my life," said Professor Pearl in acknowledging his son's death as a reason for dialogue. He is president of the Daniel Pearl Foundation, founded largely to promote cross-cultural understanding. Professor Pearl received a bachelor of science degree in electrical engineering from the Technion in Haifa, Israel, in 1960, a master's degree in physics from Rutgers University in 1965, and a PhD degree in electrical engineering from the Polytechnic Institute of Brooklyn in 1965.

Jonathan Sacks is Chief Rabbi of the United Hebrew Congregations of the Commonwealth. Appointed to this position in 1991, he is the sixth incumbent since 1845. Educated at Gonville and Caius College, Cambridge, where he obtained first class honors in philosophy, Rabbi Sacks pursued postgraduate studies at New College, Oxford, and King's College, London. Rabbi Sacks has been Visiting Professor of Philosophy at the university of Essex, Sherman Lecturer at Manchester University, Riddell Lecturer at Newcastle University, Cook Lecturer at the universities of Oxford, Edinburgh, and St Andrews, and Visiting Professor at the Hebrew University, Jerusalem. He is currently Visiting Professor of Theology at Kings' College London. In September 2001, the Archbishop of Canterbury conferred on him a Doctorate of Divinity in recognition of his first ten years in the Chief Rabbinate. He is author of *The Dignity of Difference* (Continuum, 2003), *The Politics of Hope* (Jonathan Cape, 1997), *Celebrating Life* (Continuum, 2004) *Arguments for the Sake of Heaven* (Jason Aronson, 1991),

Faith in the Future (Darton, Longman and Todd, 1995), *A Letter in the Scroll* (Free Press, 2000), *From Optimism to Hope: Thoughts for the Day* (Continuum, 2004), and other books. *The Daily Telegraph* wrote of *The Dignity of Difference* that it "stands far above other books about globalization and the so-called clash of civilizations, both for what it has to say and for the grace with which it says it."

Sir Ravi Shankar is among the world's best-known and most widely loved and respected musicians. Trained in India on the sitar under guru Baba Allaudin Khan, he collaborated famously with the Beatles in the 1960s, and afterward with the late Lord Yehudi Menuhin, Jean-Pierre Rampal, Philip Glass, and several other renowned Western musicians. Lord Menuhin paid him this tribute: "Ravi Shankar has brought me a precious gift, and through him I have added a new dimension to my experience of music. To me, his genius and his humanity can only be compared to that of Mozart's." Sir Ravi is an honorary member of the American Academy of Arts and Letters and a member of the United Nations International Rostrum of composers. He has received many awards from India and elsewhere throughout the world, including 14 doctorates, the Padma Vibhushan, Desikottam, the Magsaysay Award from Manila, three Grammy awards, the Fukuoka Grand Prize from Japan, and the Crystal Award from Davos, with the title "Global Ambassador." In 1986 he was nominated as a member of the Rajya Sabha, India's upper house of Parliament. He has been granted an honorary knighthood by the Queen of England. Now in his eighties, Sir Ravi continues to tour the world playing sitar with family members and other musicians.

Tamara Sonn is the Kenan Professor of Religion and Professor of Humanities at the College of William and Mary. Her areas of specialization are Islamic intellectual history and Islam in the contemporary world. Professor Sonn's books include *Between Qur'an and Crown: The Challenge of Political Legitimacy in the Arab World* (Westview, 1990), *Interpreting Islam* (Oxford, 1996), *Islam and the Question of Minorities* (Scholars Press, 1996), *Comparing Religions* *through Law: Judaism and Islam,* with J. Neusner (Routledge 1999), and *Judaism and Islam in Practice,* with J. Neusner and J. Brockopp (Routledge, 2000). She has also written numerous book chapters and articles, as well as entries in the *Oxford Encyclopedia of the Modern Islamic World* and *Colliers Encyclopedia.* Dr Sonn has lectured in Europe, the Middle East, Africa, and Asia. She is a member of the board of directors of the American Council for the Study of Islamic Societies and former vice-president of the Eastern Division of the American Academy of Religion. She has a BA in Philosophy from the University of Santa Clara, an MA in Philosophy from the University of Toronto, and a PhD from the University of Chicago in Near Eastern Languages and Civilizations.

Dame Marilyn Strathern is William Wyse Professor of Social Anthropology at Cambridge University and Mistress of Girton College. She is internationally renowned for her research on gender, society, kinship, new reproductive technologies, and intellectual property rights. Much of her fieldwork has been done in Papua New Guinea and England. She became interested in anthropology by reading Rousseau and visiting archaeological sites in southern Britain as a schoolgirl; soon after, she received her Bachelor's, Master's and PhD in anthropology at Cambridge University. In 1971 she published *Self-Decoration in Mount Hagen* (Duckworth), and the following year wrote *Women in Between* (Seminar Press, 1972). In 1976, Dame Marilyn was awarded the Rivers Memorial Medal from the Royal Anthropological Institute, and in 2003 she received the Wenner Gren Institute's Viking Medal, awarded to an exceptional anthropologist for lifetime achievement. From 1985 until 1993, she was Chair of the Department of Social Anthropology at the University of Manchester. In the 1990s she published five books: *Partial Connections, After Nature* (Cambridge University Press, 1992), *Reproducing the Future* (Routledge, 1992), *Technologies of Procreation* (with four co-authors, Routledge, 1999), and *Property, Substance, and Effect* (Athlone, 1999). In 1996, the American Academy of Arts and Sciences named her an Honorary Foreign Member.

Prince El Hassan bin Talal is the former Crown Prince of Jordan. He was born in Amman in 1947, youngest son of the then Crown Prince Talal bin Abdullah and Princess Zein El Sharaf bint Jamil, later King Talal and Queen Zein El Sharaf. He is the younger brother of His Majesty the late King Hussein. Their branch of the Hashemite family is the forty-second generation in direct descent from the Prophet Muhammad. He has developed a distinguished record for his work on interfaith dialogue. In 1994, His Royal Highness established the Royal Institute for Inter-Faith Studies in Jordan, and in 1999, at the seventh World Assembly of the World Conference on Religion and Peace (WCRP), held in Amman, Prince El Hassan was named Moderator of the WCRP. He is the author of seven books and numerous articles. His books include *A Study on Jerusalem* (Longman, 1979), *Palestinian Self-Determination* (Quarter Books, 1981), *Search for Peace* (St Martin's Press, 1984), *Christianity in the Arab World* (Continuum, 1994), *Continuity, Innovation and Change* (Majlis El Hassan, 2001), and *In Memory of Faisal I: The Iraqi Question* (2003). His Royal Highness was invested as Crown Prince to the Hashemite Throne of Jordan in 1965. He served as the King's closest political advisor, confidant, and deputy, as well as acting as Regent in the King's absence from the country.

Shashi Tharoor is Under-Secretary-General for Communications and Public Information of the United Nations. He was born in London in 1956 and educated in India (BA in History, St Stephen's College) and the United States, where he received a PhD at age 22 from Tufts University. He has worked for the UN since 1978. He first served the UN on the staff of the High Commissioner for Refugees, heading the Singapore office during the "boat people" crisis. Since 1989 he has been a senior official at the UN in New York, where, until late 1996, he was responsible for peacekeeping operations in the former Yugoslavia. From 1997 to 1998 he was executive assistant to UN Secretary-General Kofi Annan. In 1998 he was appointed Director of Communications and Special Projects in the office of the Secretary-General. In 2001 he was appointed by the Secretary-General as interim head of the Department of Public Information, and was confirmed as

Under-Secretary-General in 2002. Dr Tharoor is the author of numerous articles, short stories, and commentaries, and the winner of several journalism and literary awards. His books include *Reasons of State* (Advent Books, 1981), *The Great Indian Novel* (Penguin, 1989), and *Riot* (Arcade, 2002). His novel, *Show Business* (Arcade, 1993), which received a front-page accolade from *The New York Times Book Review*, was made into the 1997 motion picture *Bollywood*.

Archbishop Desmond Tutu won the Nobel Peace Prize in 1984 for his role as a unifying leader in the campaign to resolve the apartheid problem in South Africa. The Nobel Committee emphasized the significance of the nonviolent aspect of his work for liberation, "a struggle in which black and white South Africans unite to bring their country out of conflict and crisis." He was born in 1931 in Transvaal and educated in Johannesburg, graduating from the University of South Africa in 1954. After three years as a high school teacher, he began studying theology and was ordained a priest in 1960. He devoted the years 1962–6 to further theological study in England, leading to a Master of Theology degree. From 1967 to 1972 he taught theology in South Africa before returning to England for three years as the assistant director of a theological institute in London. In 1975 he was appointed Dean of St Mary's Cathedral in Johannesburg, the first black to hold that position. From 1976 to 1978 he was Bishop of Lesotho, and in 1978 became the first black General Secretary of the South African Council of Churches. Tutu is an honorary doctor of a number of leading universities in the USA, Britain, and Germany. He has written several books, including *No Future without Forgiveness* (Image, 2000) and *God Has a Dream: A Vision of Hope for Our Time* (Doubleday, 2004).

William L. Ury is Director of the Harvard University Law School Global Negotiation Project. Author of numerous books and articles on the negotiation process, he works as a consultant and mediator with community, government, and business leaders around the world. Professor Ury's research focuses on the global dynamics of transforming destructive conflicts into constructive processes. Through his "Third Side" initiative, he has examined the role the community can play in preventing, resolving, and containing destructive conflict. His work includes dispute systems design and prevention of or response to ethnic conflict. One of his recent projects is the global e-Parliament, whose mission is to further global democracy through the creation of an ongoing forum in which the world's democratically elected legislators can engage with civil society in a joint search for effective solutions to global problems. Professor Ury also serves as a member of the International Negotiation Network headed by former President Jimmy Carter, Dayle Spencer, and William Spencer. Co-author of the internationally acclaimed *Getting to YES* (Penguin, 1981, 1991), his more recent books include *The Third Side* (Penguin, 2000) and *Must We Fight?* (Jossey-Bass, 2002).

Sergio Vieira de Mello was the United Nations High Commissioner for Human Rights from September 12, 2002, until August 19, 2003, when he was tragically killed in Iraq. He dealt successfully with some of the UN's most vexing humanitarian and peacekeeping challenges, from fashioning refugee protection and resettlement schemes for Vietnamese refugees to overseeing the repatriation of 300,000 Cambodian refugees from Thailand, setting up a UN civil administration in Kosovo, and managing the political transition in East Timor. He was renowned for his extraordinary intelligence and judgment, graciousness and wit, and profound dedication to humanitarian principles. Born in Rio de Janeiro in 1948, Mr de Mello joined the UN in 1969 while studying philosophy and humanities at the University of Paris (Panthéon-Sorbonne). He spent most of his career working for the UN High Commissioner for Refugees in Geneva, served in humanitarian and peacekeeping operations in Bangladesh, Sudan, Cyprus, Mozambique, and Peru, and in 1998 was appointed Under-Secretary-General for Humanitarian Affairs and Emergency Relief Coordinator. In May 2003, he was asked by the Secretary-General to take a four-month leave of absence to serve in Iraq as Special Representative of the Secretary-General. Among his last words: "Don't let them pull the UN out of Iraq. Don't let them fail this mission."

Jody Williams is an international activist for peace and humanitarian relief. She was awarded the Nobel Peace Prize in 1997 for her extraordinary accomplishments in clearing anti-personnel mines from battle zones the world over and for humanitarian relief efforts in Central America and elsewhere. Founding coordinator of the International Campaign to Ban Landmines, she oversaw the growth of the ICBL to more than 1,300 nongovernmental organizations in over 85 countries and served as the chief strategist and spokesperson for the campaign. Working in an unprecedented cooperation with governments, UN bodies, and the International Committee of the Red Cross, the ICBL achieved its goal of an international treaty banning anti-personnel landmines during the diplomatic conference held in Oslo in September 1997. Ms Williams now serves as Campaign Ambassador for the ICBL, speaking on its behalf all over the world. She has a Master's degree in international relations from The Johns Hopkins School of Advanced International Studies (1984), a Master's degree in teaching Spanish and ESL from the School for International Training in Vermont (1976), and a Bachelor of Arts degree from the University of Vermont (1972).

Edward O. Wilson is the Pellegrino University Research Professor and Honorary Curator in Entomology at Harvard University. He is widely regarded as the father of biodiversity and sociobiology, the study of nature's role in shaping human behavior. Professor Wilson's research has spanned the spectrum from specialist to generalist on a grand scale, starting with his path-breaking research on ants and moving eventually to the biological basis of morality and an overarching theory of concilience in the natural world. Winner of two Pulitzer prizes for nonfiction works, *On Human Nature* (Harvard University Press, 1988) and *The Ants* (with B. Holldobler; Belknap Press, 1990), Professor Wilson has also authored *Concilience* (Vintage, 1998), *The Diversity of Life* (W. W. Norton, 1993), *The Future of Life* (Vintage, 2003), and other major works on biology. His book *Sociobiology* (Belknap, 1975) not only created a stir in its own right in describing evolutionary forces behind social characteristics of organisms, but also spawned the field of evolutionary psychology in the 1990s. Professor Wilson has written that the spiritual impulse is both an evolutionary advantage central to human nature and a key to hope for the future.

James D. Wolfensohn is President of the World Bank and Chairman of the Bank's Board of Executive Directors. Appointed in 1995, following a distinguished career as an international investment banker involved in development issues and the global environment, he presides over the Bank's five affiliated international development organizations. He has traveled to over 100 countries to understand first hand the challenges facing the World Bank and its 184 member countries. In the process, he has initiated strategic partnerships between the Bank and the governments it serves, the private sector, civil society, regional development banks, and the UN. Mr Wolfensohn chaired the board of New York's Carnegie Hall from 1980 to 1991, and from 1990 to 1996 chaired the board of trustees of the John F. Kennedy Center for the Performing Arts in Washington, DC. Born in Australia in 1933, Mr Wolfensohn is a naturalized US citizen. He holds a BA and an LLB from the University of Sydney and an MBA from Harvard. Mr Wolfensohn was a member of the 1956 Australian Olympic Fencing Team. He is a Fellow of the American Academy of Arts and Sciences and the American Philosophical Society. In 1995, he was awarded an Honorary Knighthood by Queen Elizabeth II for his contribution to the arts.

Part I
Introduction

1

Toward a More Civil Twenty-first Century

Akbar Ahmed and Brian Forst

The events of September 11, 2001, forced people all over the world to confront a dramatically changing and dangerous world. It also forced the two of us, as social scientists and concerned citizens, to confront some central questions:

- What does it mean to absorb and move forward from an event like the terrorist attack of 9/11?
- How are we to make sense of the changes and the coming time?
- What are the main global ideas that explain the confused landscape?
- Where is the hatred coming from?
- How can we challenge the despair and gloom engendered by the idea of an unending night of clash and conflict?

Colleagues and then friends working on campus, we developed the idea of inviting some of the most prominent figures of our time to ponder these questions. We wanted to hear from other scholars, but also from public figures and religious leaders from different continents and a variety of cultures, religions, and ethnic traditions, raised under different economic and political systems, schooled in different scholarly disciplines and having excelled in different callings – in the tradition of exploratory, cross-disciplinary research. We were interested as scholars in making sense of the course of events set in motion in 2001; we are more than interested as parents and grandfathers in finding a way to spread global sanity.

In the chapters that follow, we present the thinking that emerged from this enterprise. We asked the essayists[1] to look into their diverse and rich experiences to find a range of prospects for positive engagement among cultures and civilizations, to help us all return to the trajectory of dialogue, cross-cultural exchange, and mutual understanding among civilizations that has in fact been under way for centuries, to offer their visions for a vibrant future, to enrich us all. We were more than pleased with the extraordinary group of people who agreed to contribute to this project, and then with the breadth and thoughtfulness of their contributions. The essays fell along a path that traces the nature and sources of the conflict, alternative approaches for dealing with it, and the idea that we need not take passive bystander roles as the future unfolds.

Central Themes Raised in the Essays

The contributors to this book do not see eye to eye on every matter; they reveal a divergence of opinion about what is important and what is not. They are unanimous on one point, however: they all see viable alternative scenarios to a clash of civilizations for the twenty-first century. Their essays offer an array of ideas on the nature of the problems we confront and how to manage them to produce a more robust future. None supported the premise central to Professor Samuel P. Huntington's clash of civilizations theory that the creation of enemies is essential to cultural identity,[2] and several suggested that many trends throughout the world suggest a convergence of basic values and interests.

Dealing with underlying causes of conflict

The essayists see the most significant prospects for progress in interventions against the factors that contribute to tension, conflict, and pessimism throughout the world: intolerance, poverty, discrimination, illiteracy, autocratic and tyrannical rulers, globalism, alienation that typically follows each and all of these factors, and the misappropriation of religion for political purposes.

The source of conflict and alienation most commonly cited by the essayists is *intolerance* and hatred. For Rajmohan Gandhi, intolerance was a personal experience of his youth, spent in a setting of mutual enmity between Hindus and Muslims, and he has seen such tragedies of intolerance played out again and again in the Middle East, Africa, and many other places throughout the world. Queen Noor of Jordan, also intimately familiar with at least two cultures, finds intolerance embedded in virtually every culture, and often least visible to the intolerant. She adds that intolerance too often leads to the feeling of entitlement to use force, making for a cycle of fear, intolerance, and violence. Diana Eck tells of the tragic fallout of intolerance as reflected in dialogue among women of several faiths: Muslim, Hindu and Sikh, Christian and Jewish.

For the late Sergio Vieira de Mello, intolerance is especially pernicious, because it so often hides behind dishonesty and pretext. He sees the rule of law as key to securing human rights and providing a formal infrastructure for the promotion and preservation of tolerance. He suggests that the expansion of tolerance might begin with women, who are a force for peace, the glue that binds family and community.

Others focus on the sources of intolerance. Rabbi Jonathan Sacks observes that religion is often erroneously regarded as the source of intolerance, that the seeds of intolerance lie more fundamentally in exclusivism, fear, and ignorance.[3] Judea Pearl takes exception to a simple exclusivist explanation, observing that it is flawed with an incurable contradiction: even inclusivists must separate themselves from those who advocate intolerance to different cultures and faiths, who threaten the survival of mankind, and who trample on basic norms of civilized society. Shashi Tharoor notes that intolerance cannot be solved through censorship; he sees the media as a common instrument of fear and intolerance, but no less as an instrument with a proven ability to promote tolerance, reminding us of the power of media as an early warning system on the abuse of human rights. For Kofi Annan, poverty and illiteracy are prime sources of intolerance, and the challenge is to reinvigorate the fight against intolerance through legal measures, education, economic and social development – before the intolerance gets played out on the battlefield. Zbigniew Brzezinski sees an important source of today's intolerance in an imbalance of power that is being neutralized by access to large-scale lethality and exacerbated by a United States foreign policy that has been insensitive to essential nuances of the global landscape. Jody Williams writes, along a parallel line, that enmities have been inflamed by a "war on terror" that has weakened global security in the name of protecting it. Walter Isaacson offers a morality tale to suggest a more effective antidote to intolerance: he recalls Benjamin Franklin's skillful handling of religious intolerance through tolerance and religious pluralism, mixed with touches of humor and humility.

Several of the essayists emphasize *poverty* and alienation as dominant factors behind tension and conflict. Sergio Vieira de Mello regards equality and dignity as basic universal values and finds serious lapses in the world's commitment to those values, noting that extreme poverty has marginalized some 1.5 billion people. James D. Wolfensohn writes that the vast majority of the world's population live in developing countries, and families have been seriously disrupted by the migration of countless workers to foreign lands in search of jobs. Shashi Tharoor observes that the poor fall further behind as the rest of the world climbs aboard the communication and information technology boom, noting that the 400,000 citizens of the tiny nation of Luxembourg have access to more internet bandwidth than the 760 million inhabitants of the African continent. The world has never been inhabited by so many poor people, and while their access to information lags far behind that of the affluent, never before have the poor been so exposed to the contrast between their plight and the seemingly unattainable heights of wealth and opportunity available to people in other parts of the world.

The role of religion

Is the clash of civilizations a product of religion? Edward O. Wilson argues that it most certainly is, that "tragic conflicts make it clear that religious dogmas are no longer adequate guides." He grants that religion has enriched cultures with some of their best attributes, including the ideals of altruism, public service, and aesthetics in the arts, but adds that it has also validated tribal myths that are "forever and dangerously divisive." Noting provocatively that the sacred texts of the Abrahamic faiths speak on behalf of "archaic patriarchies in the parched Middle East," Wilson sees the scientific illuminations of enlightened people offering a more transparent and reliable basis for understanding, in a manner that transcends cultural difference and unites humanity. If religion gave humans a Darwinian edge in Paleolithic times, rational thinking and proved knowledge should give the edge today.

Several of the contributors offer a more nuanced and charitable view of religion. Judea Pearl notes that ancient scriptures provide us with intellectual resources, not complete recipes for moral behavior. Bishop Desmond Tutu observes that religion can produce saints or rogues, that it is healthy when transcendent and malignant when caught up in finding infidels and adversaries. He notes that all the major religions produce rogues, yet all emphasize fundamental moral values of honesty, fidelity in marriage, compassion, the unity of humankind, and peace – a point that does not play as well on prime-time television as reports on the latest acts of "radical fundamentalists." Kofi Annan helps us to understand about rogues in observing that religious concerns too often become wrongfully entangled in political and territorial issues. Rabbi Sacks also sees the capacity for religions to create conflicts across borders, but sees religions primarily as institutions that bind people to one another and to God, giving them an identity and a moral compass that values peace and brotherhood. James Wolfensohn adds that faith-based organizations are a powerful tool in the world's fight against poverty and the problems associated with poverty. Prince El Hassan bin Talal observes that the prospects for a peaceful "melting pot" planet are enhanced when each religion is capable of recognizing our interdependence, respecting pluralism and difference, and celebrating our common humanity.

Expanding dialogue

In 1998, President Khatami of Iran proposed a "dialogue among civilizations" at the United Nations. Two years later, also at the UN, he elaborated on the idea by basing the proposal on both cultural and religious elements: Persian thought and culture, born at the crossroads of "political hurricanes as well as pleasant breezes of cultural exchange and also venues for international trade," and "Islamic emphasis on essential human equality and its disdain for such elements as birth and blood," enriched by a "plurality derived from the diversity of responses evoked after Islam reached various nations." The essayists in this volume endorse this spirit: they refer repeatedly to dialogue as the vastly superior alternative to conflict among civilizations.[4] Bernard Lewis reminds us that dialogue is as old as history itself, that in dialogue there is hope, and in clash an unending pattern of attack and counterattack. Lord Carey (the former Archbishop of Canterbury) points out that some of the most potentially lethal problems are between the West and Islam, and that effective dialogue here must confront deeply held grievances, and must do so honestly and responsibly. Kofi Annan adds that dialogue is the antidote to intolerance and conflict, that it can help to disentangle religion from politics and open the way to understanding, cooperation, and the expansion of human rights – but not when it gets bogged down in inflammatory rhetoric, the common precursor to hostile acts. In a similar vein, President Khatami of Iran observes that effective dialogue begins with listening.

Dialogue inevitably involves a discussion of commonalities and differences, and Marilyn Strathern's essay attends to one of the paradoxes in this domain: How can one resolve the tension between the moral responsibility to see differences among essentially similar people with one's moral responsibility to acknowledge fundamental similarities among people who are clearly different? As the title of her essay suggests, the solution lies in a serviceable old metaphor. In a related vein, Ravi Shankar notes that effective dialogue requires that one be in tune with oneself before trying to fine-tune another, that dialogue works best when it is conducted without prejudice, grounded in spirituality. In recalling his path-breaking musical dialogues with celebrities as different as the Beatles' George Harrison and violinist Lord Yehudi Menuhin, he echoes a theme raised by Annan: Diversity enriches dialogue.

Amitai Etzioni states that if transnational dialogue is to shape public policy for the better, it cannot be based on the shaping of public opinion through the use of Madison Avenue devices. Other essayists amplify Etzioni's point. Queen Noor emphasizes the importance of *respect*, noting that progress is impossible without respectful dialogue. Tamara Sonn gives a stirring account of a series of respectful dialogues between Judea Pearl, father of slain *Wall Street Journal* reporter Daniel Pearl, and Akbar Ahmed, one of the two editors of this volume. She observes that dialogue does not provide instant gratification of the sort offered by violent strikes of vengeance, but it may create something ultimately more powerful: the goodwill needed to secure peace. Rabbi Sacks reminds us not to lose sight of the goal: in dialogue, the hero is one who turns an enemy into a friend. He adds that to open the door for such a result it may be necessary to find the moral courage to forgive.

A few note that even in the face of conflict, dialogue can and should be pursued as a complementary intervention, one that can serve to expedite an end to the conflict. Jean Bethke Elshtain, for one, observes that a prerequisite to forcible intervention is dialogue within civilizations, needed for critical reflection on one's own motives and deeds, to ensure that the use of force is truly just. She adds that when war follows such reflection, the just war principle keeps alive the possibility of dialogue to nurture the prospects of mutual understanding and peace.

The urgent need for dialogue and positive cultural exchange among civilizations is suggested by the fact that people in the West today tend to know very much about Osama bin Laden and almost nothing at all about Muslims and Islam, while Muslims have similarly distorted views of Westerners generally, and Americans in particular. These mutual misperceptions have been revealed in numerous polls taken both in the West and among Muslim populations.

Improving governance

Another major theme is the too-common problem of poor governance and the need to improve it. Sergio Vieira de Mello observes that more countries are democratic today than ever before, but that democracy is no guarantee against the hubris that leads to brutality, expansionism, and war. He adds that where governments cannot promote the expansion of human rights and dignity, those interests should be promoted "from below," using the resources of corporate citizenship. Isaacson notes that a key to effective governance is the art of compromise; while unheroic, it can be crucial to the making of a democracy. Benjamin Barber observes that governments must be sensitive to increasing global interdependencies; when they are not, citizens can and will take action on their own, often through non-governmental organizations bound together through international civic cooperation. Joseph Nye emphasizes the need for nations to replace traditional hard-power emphases on the carrots and sticks of assertive foreign policy with soft-power emphases on exemplary action and genuine interest in listening, acts that reveal legitimacy and mutual respect.

These prospects – confronting the poverty, illiteracy, fear, and other sources of conflict, expanding and improving techniques for dialogue, improving government, expanding civic engagements, and so on – are helpful, and this list is by no means exhaustive. We still have much more to learn about the sources of conflict and the effectiveness of alternative interventions for dealing with them. Many other creative solutions to the problems we confront await discovery, and we will do well to be creative and persistent in finding them.

Several pathways for further development are clear, including the promotion of constitutional democratic initiatives that emphasize the rule of law and basic human rights, in order to stimulate initiatives that will strengthen the voices of moderation and civility in all civilizations. Support of such governmental infrastructures can lead to more effective public education programs, equal rights for women, creation and reinforcement of positive social networks that build trust, limits on the exports of entertainments that glamorize violence, creation of inducements to cross-cultural collaboration, research on dialogue – to learn what sorts of dialogue settings and formats work best to build mutual understanding, tolerance, respect, and cooperation – and perhaps most important, launching these initiatives with humility, mindful of the need to respect traditions and institutions that resist such efforts.

The Imperative of Action

The essayists remark that the challenges are great and many, but that the alternative of mindlessly conceding to conflict is no longer acceptable. William Ury invites us to shift from being passive observers to becoming responsible participants in a web of "Third Siders." Queen Noor asks that moderates become more passionate about the need to rein in the forces of simple-minded solutions grounded in inflamed fears and intolerance. Jody Williams, quoting the poet Roethke, invites us to specialize in the impossible. Martin Marty, quoting Abraham Lincoln's call for the better angels of our nature, asks that we try tolerance, that we counter intolerance, and that we even go so far as risking hospitality.

The essays that follow speak to the power of dialogue and mutual understanding, to notions of tolerance, respect, cooperation, and commitment. In sharing their personal experiences of the superiority of positive engagements with people of different cultures and interests, they make clear the prospect of a future to which we can look forward, the possibility of a world in which people appreciate the diversities that make us interesting collectively and the sentiments and interests we have in common. As scholars we are also perennial students, and these people have filled our table with a sumptuous banquet of food for thought. They have given us major elements for the development of a blueprint for the preservation of humanity.

Uppermost is our hope that these essays will do more than make for fascinating reading. We will regard this project as a success if it moves the reader to a sense of purpose, a realization that each of us is in a position, however small or large, to shift the collective awareness away from the nightmare of Apocalypse and make real the prospect of seeking out and nurturing our common humanity, while celebrating our own uniqueness and the uniqueness of others.

Notes

1   While a few of the essays were adapted from prior material of the contributors, all were crafted for this collection by the authors except for one, that of Sergio Vieira de Mello, who was tragically killed in a terrorist attack on the United Nations headquarters in Baghdad in 2003. We received permission from the United Nations to excerpt his essay from a speech he gave in London in November 2002.

2   Huntington, *The Clash of Civilizations and the Remaking of World Order* (New York: Simon and Schuster, 1996), p. 20.

3   See also Sacks's book, *The Dignity of Difference: How to Avoid the Clash of Civilizations* (London: Continuum Press, 2003).

4   One of us has written extensively that dialogue is a vastly superior alternative to conflict: dialogue both within and between civilizations, dialogue that is sane and balanced, dialogue that is inclusive, elevating an interest in listening and learning over a tendency to express the "we are right and others are wrong" point of view (Ahmed, *Islam under Siege: Living Dangerously in a Post-Honor World* (Cambridge: Polity, 2003), pp. 21, 48, 143, 165, 171).

Part II

The Nature and Sources of the Problem

2

The Simple Power of Weakness, the Complex Vulnerability of Power

Zbigniew Brzezinski

The notion of total security is now a myth. Total security and total defense in the age of globalization are not attainable. The real issue is: With how much insecurity can we live while protecting our interests in an increasingly interactive, interdependent world? Insecurity, while uncomfortable, has been the fate of many nations for centuries. For America there is no longer a choice: even if socially disagreeable, its insecurity has to be politically manageable – and that requires a clear, coherent articulation of the threat America faces.

Given that America is a democracy, the definition of the threat must be easily understood by the public, so that it can sustain the material sacrifices needed to address the threat. That puts a premium on clarity and specificity, but it also creates the temptation of demagogy. If the threat can be personalized, identified as evil, and even stereotyped visually, social mobilization for a long-haul effort becomes easier. In human affairs, and especially in international affairs, hate and prejudice are much more powerful emotions than sympathy or affinity. They are also easier to express than a more authentic appraisal of the inevitably complex historical and political motives that influence the conduct of nations and even of terrorist groupings. But resorting to demagogy

to exploit these emotions hinders genuine public understanding
of the threat and how best to overcome it.

The Dangers of Demagogy

Public discourse in the United States after September 11, 2001,
highlights this problem. The public reaction – as reflected in
speeches by leading politicians as well as editorials in the leading
publications – has tended to focus primarily on terrorism as such,
emphasizing its evil character and concentrating attention on the
notorious personality of Osama bin Laden. President Bush was
inclined to treat the threat almost in theological terms, viewing
it as a collision between "good and evil." He even embraced the
Leninist formula that "he who is not with us is against us," a notion
that is always congenial to an aroused public mood, but whose
black-and-white view of the world ignores the shades of gray that
define most global dilemmas.

President Bush's largely theological approach, in addition to
its politically mobilizing effect, had the added tactical advantage
of conflating into one simple formula several sources of the
threat, irrespective of whether they were interconnected or not.
The famous presidential reference to the "axis of evil," made in
early 2002, rhetorically lumped together the separate challenges
posed by North Korea to the stability of Northeast Asia, by Iran's
longer-range ambitions in the Persian Gulf region, and by the
unfinished legacy of the 1991 campaign against Iraq's Saddam
Hussein. The increasingly ominous dilemmas inherent in these
states' efforts to acquire nuclear weaponry were thus encapsulated
by the moral condemnation of three specific but not allied regimes
(two of them in fact mutual enemies) and were linked to the
American people's painful and immediate experience with direct
terrorism.

For the American people, the "axis of evil" will probably suffice
for a while as a rough definition of the threat. The problem that
arises, however, is twofold. First, since America's security is now
linked to global security and the campaign against terrorism
requires global support, it is important that others, outside

America, share this definition. Will they? Second, is such a definition adequate in its diagnosis, and does it provide an effective
basis for a long-term and successful strategic response to the challenge posed both separately as well as jointly by terrorism and the
proliferation of weapons of mass destruction?

The difficulty is that the administration's definition of what or
whom Americans are being asked to fight in "the war on terrorism" has been articulated in a remarkably vague fashion. Matters
have not been clarified by the President's reduction (or elevation,
depending on one's vantage point) of terrorists to "evildoers,"
otherwise unidentified, whose motivations are said to be
simply satanic. Identifying terrorism itself as the enemy also
blithely ignored the fact that terrorism is a lethal technique
for intimidation employed by individuals, groups, and states.
One does not wage a war against a technique or a tactic.
No one, for instance, would have declared at the outset of the
Second World War that the war was being fought against
"blitzkrieg."

In truth, terrorism is a complex phenomenon – its roots are
manifold, as are the means needed to address them. Terrorism
rooted in ethnic, national, or religious resentments is the most
enduring and the least susceptible to simple extirpation. Generally speaking, terrorism derived from social grievances, even if
ideologically reinforced by a dogma such as radical Marxism, tends
to fade if the societies in question fail to embrace the terrorists'
cause. Social isolation eventually demoralizes some of the terrorists and exposes others to capture. Terrorism based more specifically on the support of an alienated and geographically remote
social class, such as peasantry, has shown a greater endurance (as
the experiences of China and Latin America demonstrate), particularly if backed by a guerrilla movement. But terrorism derived
from shared ethnicity backed by historic myths and fired by
religious zeal has proven to be the most resistant of all to simple
physical suppression.

The terrorists themselves are doubtless irredeemable, but the
conditions that foster them may not be so. This is an important
distinction. Terrorists tend to live in a world of their own,
cocooned within their pathological self-righteousness. Violence

becomes not just the means to an end but also their *raison d'être*. That is why their elimination is necessary. To make certain their ranks are not replenished, however, a careful political strategy is needed in order to weaken the complex political and cultural forces that give rise to terrorism. What creates them has to be politically undercut.

The Power of Weakness

It is crucial also to note a distinctive dimension of the threat: it emanates not from the strong, but from the weak. On September 11, nineteen fanatics – armed merely with some box-cutters and a willingness to forfeit their own lives – managed directly or indirectly to militarize US foreign policy, accelerate Russia's Western reorientation, eventually prompt growing fissures between America and Europe, intensify America's economic malaise, and alter the traditional American definition of civil rights. Never before had so much pain been inflicted on so power-ful many by so impotent few.

Therein lies the dilemma for the world's only superpower: how to cope with an enemy that is physically weak but endowed with a fanatical motivation. Unless the sources of the motivation are diluted, attempts to thwart and eliminate the enemy will be to no avail. Hatred will breed replenishment. The foe can be eliminated only through a sensitive recognition of motives and passions that are not precisely defined.

The fanatical weak cannot transform themselves into the strong, but they have the power to make the lives of the domi-nant increasingly miserable. The power of weakness is the political equivalent of what military strategists have labeled asym-metrical warfare. In effect, the revolution in military affairs – which maximizes the physical power of the technologically dominant – is being offset by a quantum leap in social vulnerability, increasing the fear that the powerful have of the weak.

Unlike the weak, the powerful cannot afford the luxury of over-simplification. They become weak by oversimplifying their fears.

Because their interests are broad, because their stakes are inter-dependent, and because for them the definition of the good life is subjectively and objectively wide-ranging, the powerful must not simply demonize the challenge posed by the weak or reduce it to a unidimensional scale. To do so is to risk focusing only on the superficial manifestations of the challenge, while ignoring its more complex and historically rooted impulses. The weak can fight "the Great Satan" because simplicity of focus helps to com-pensate for their weakness. The powerful, on the contrary, must understand and confront the enemy's complexity.

From Domination to Leadership

There is thus a practical dimension to the seamless dilemmas of global disorder that America now faces. Power and force alone are not sufficient to preserve American hegemony, because America's foes are zealous, less attached to their lives, and ready to exploit America's democratic principles without compunction. Coercion creates new antagonists but does little to prevent them from slipping through the crevices of democracy and attacking from within. If the United States wants to retain the life and liberty it cherishes inside the country, it must maintain the legitimacy of its predominance outside the country. That means nothing less than genuine cooperation with allies, not merely the support of supplicants, and it means above all else a sustained cooperative effort to grasp the complicated nature of the contemporary global disorder.

Accordingly, America should define its security in ways that help mobilize the self-interest of others. Ultimately, it is in America's national security interest that the Muslim believers come to see themselves as just as much a part of the emerging global community as the currently more prosperous and democ-ratic non-Islamic regions of the world. It is equally important that the politically active elements in the Islamic world not view the United States as the principal obstacle to Islam's civilizational rebirth, as the main sponsor of their socially regressive and eco-nomically self-serving political elites, or as the supporter of foreign states that seek to perpetuate or restore a quasi-colonial subordination of various Muslim peoples.

It is essential that Muslim moderates isolate Muslim extremists. A more peaceful world is simply not attainable without the constructive participation of the world's 1.2 billion Muslims. Only a highly differentiated US policy, responsive to the reality of Muslim diversity, can promote that desirable, if still distant, objective.

More generally, American leadership can be sustained more effectively if the world understands that the trajectory of America's grand strategy is toward a global community of shared interests. American power and America's worldwide social seductiveness, working together, could promote the gradual emergence of such a community. They could illuminate the world with the hope of human progress. Misused and in collision, however, they could push the world into chaos while leaving America beleaguered. An anxious America, obsessed with its own security, could find itself isolated in the world, the focus of global hatred. In the end, which scenario prevails hinges on a simple choice: Will America seek to dominate the world, or lead it?

3

Dialogue and the Echo Boom of Terror: Religious Women's Voices after 9/11

Diana L. Eck

"As an American and as a Muslim, I was horrified to watch the television that morning. I felt as if pieces of myself were tumbling off of those buildings. All the work we had been doing for years and years to build up positive relations between Muslims and other faiths seemed to be falling and crumbling." Sharifa Alkhateeb of the North American Council for Muslim Women opened our day of intensive discussion in New York, just six weeks after September 11. Sharifa's fear that the positive work of interfaith relations would suffer a cataclysmic setback was a working hypothesis. The preceding six weeks had been filled with the backlash of terror for Muslims and Sikhs, South Asians and Arabs, in the United States.

The leaders of American Women's Religious Networks had met once before, gathered together by the Pluralism Project at Harvard University. We had met in Cambridge for two sunny days in April of 2001 to get to know each other's organizations and to connect our circles of work. It was a process of mutual learning, exploring the boundaries and recognizing women's leadership in a world of interfaith relations too often dominated by the publicly visible leadership of men. We represented another reality, determined to be more visible and vocal: United Methodist Women, Women of Reform Judaism, the Jewish Orthodox Feminist Alliance, the North American Council for Muslim Women, the Muslim Women's League, Manavi, and many others. Our April meeting in Cambridge had begun to build relationships, but as we met in the wake of September 11, all of us wondered if they would be strong enough to hold the weight they now bore. Even as we gathered that November morning, we acknowledged that one of our members, a representative of Hadassah, one of the largest Jewish women's organizations, was constrained from attending by her board because of the presence of the founder and president of the Muslim Women's League. The inability to sit together at the same table, with all of the imputed views and suspicions it represented, signaled the fraying of relationships. Honest interfaith discussion of American policy in the Middle East was almost at a standstill.

By November, the term 9/11 had become its own locution, with a powerful penumbra of meanings: the blue September morning, the crumbling of the towers and the eerie images of Ground Zero, the helmeted firemen and the trucks filled with rubble, the chain-link fences covered with flowers and messages, the impromptu shrines and candles, the grief and recrimination, the faces and portraits of those who had died, printed day after day in the newspaper. Included in the penumbra of meaning conveyed by 9/11 was, by now, the reality of war in Afghanistan. The official American backlash against an evasive and unseen enemy was paralleled by an unofficial domestic backlash against neighbors in our very midst. The age-old strategy of punishment, retribution, and revenge was being enacted and tested on the domestic and international scene. Gambling on their effectiveness was the government's working hypothesis. Would the blunt instruments of war, even with their precision, root out terrorists or create the conditions for them to flourish?

Now gathered around the table in New York, each of us described, carefully and personally, what had happened to us and to the women in our communities in the weeks following September 11. We began putting together our own composite picture, assessing as best we could the "collateral damage" of September

11, both for women and for the interfaith movement more broadly. All of us had seen both the worst and the best, from our own particular vantage point of vision. All of us were aware that we were entering new terrain in interreligious relations.

Emira Habiby Browne of the Arab-American Family Support Center in New York recalled the fear that welled up as she heard the news. "I was driving downtown when I turned on the news and heard what had happened. They were already comparing it to Pearl Harbor, and my first thought was 'Oh my God, we're going to be rounded up and put in camps now.'" She described the strain of the following weeks as the Arab-American Center experienced soaring demand and unprecedented siege at the same time. The fraying of the fabric of trust was also the experience of Blu Greenberg of the Jewish Orthodox Feminist Alliance and Carolyn Kunin of Women of Reform Judaism, who described how painful it was to see the celebratory Arab street scenes broadcast on television, a searing reminder of the reality of anti-American and anti-Israel sentiment. Sister Helen Marie Burns of the Leadership Conference of Women Religious, a nationwide Catholic organization, described feelings many of us shared. "From the moment I watched the second plane hit the tower, I felt such a deep sadness. Not anger, but a deep sadness. That sadness has not left me since that day. I have been sobered at a level of my being that hasn't been touched before."

Muslim, Arab-American, and South Asian women around the table had all experienced the fear of being marked with suspicion. Laila Al-Marayati from Los Angeles spoke of the threats both her mosque and its Islamic school had received, along with an enormous and exhausting volume of requests for information, explanation, and interpretation. Shamita Das Dasgupta of Manavi, an organization focused on violence against South Asian women in the US, described new strains in a program that serves Muslim and Hindu women alike. They felt besieged from the outside, and they experienced new tensions within. "We were already struggling," said Shamita, "because domestic violence within our communities challenges our perceptions of who we are. But 9/11 has almost brought to a breaking point the relations we had built up for seventeen years between the Muslim, Hindu, and Sikh communities, between Indians and Pakistanis. Now we hear people say, 'Muslim women should not be going there.' Yet our shelter is full of Muslim women. Hindus say, 'We should not wear *selwar kamiz*, or now we should wear a *bindi* mark on our foreheads so people don't think we're Muslim.' In one sense we are now struggling against our own communities."

Navjot Kaur, a Sikh woman, recounted the growing roster of incidents that had been reported in the previous six weeks to the Sikh Mediawatch and Resource Task Force (SMART). Sikhs were targeted for their turbans, revealing the ignorance and insecurity of a country unfamiliar with its own newest citizens. There were incidents of harassment, beatings, and arson. In Mesa, Arizona, Balbir Singh Sodhi had been shot and killed, mistaken for a turbaned follower of Osama bin Laden. As Navjot put it, "While September 11 has unified the nation in many ways, it has also opened up an outlet for acceptable hate crimes against minorities. Though the violence and harassment against Sikhs is often described as a problem affecting Sikh men, it has also affected Sikh women. Some Sikh women wear turbans. Others dress in traditional *selwar kamiz*, and they are targeted for that reason. Or they are targeted just because of the color of their skin."

Beyond the unraveling of trust and the eruptions of violence, there was another important fact that emerged in sharing our experience: that incidents of brutality and violence here at home had also elicited a wave of sympathetic support in response. If there was a violent backlash to 9/11 that targeted minorities in the United States, there was also a backlash to the backlash that resoundingly rejected these acts. There was a sustained countervailing outreach, hands stretched across each chasm that opened, connecting people in spite of, and perhaps because of, the inchoate fear, anger, and sadness that spread in the aftermath of 9/11.

Emira Habiby Browne described an Arab-American security initiative in New York, developed in response to the fear of being randomly victimized. "We thought we would establish an escort system, because we heard immediately after September 11 that children were not going to school," she said. "Arab children were scared to go out, and their mothers didn't want to go out either. So we put out a notice that we wanted to start an escort system, and we had hundreds of people calling to say they wanted to participate. Eventually, we had over a thousand volunteers."

Rifle fire hit the stained glass dome of the Islamic Center of Greater Toledo on September 11, but Cherrefe Kadri told the story of the response. "A Christian radio station in the Toledo area, contacted me, wanting to do something. They called out on the airwaves for people to come together at our mosque to ring our building, and to pray for our protection." Cherrefe described how moved she was by this initiative from complete strangers. "We were hoping for 300 or 500 people and we thought that number might be able to get around the mosque. But two thousand people showed up."

Sharifa Alkhateeb summarized what for many of us had been a climate change. Her own worst fears of the collapse of initiatives for dialogue were, in fact, surprisingly undermined by the events of the subsequent weeks. "From my experience after September 11," she said, "for every one negative thing that has happened, there have been, without exaggeration, at least a hundred positive things, not the least of which is people's willingness to want to know something more about each other, something deeper, something beyond the sound bite." The hypothesis of the cataclysmic setback for interfaith relations could be sustained only if we did not try to understand those "hundred positive things." There was an echo boom from even the most violent acts: the wide community support for the family of Balbir Singh Sodhi in Mesa, Arizona, bringing thousands of people together who previously had no knowledge at all of the Sikh neighbors in their midst. The response to Hazim Barakat, an Islamic bookstore owner in Alexandria, Virginia, whose store window was shattered by bricks wrapped with messages of hate. Hundreds of people stopped by; messages and flowers flooded into his shop from neighbors he did not know, but who now reached out to him.

As the months have passed, it is clear that 9/11, far from being a setback for interfaith relations in the United States, has become a stimulus to far more serious dialogue. In November of 2001, we were just beginning to see the emergence of a new wave of interfaith initiatives across the United States. According to the research of the Pluralism Project, this has grown in significance in the months since then. Countless cities and towns – from Memphis, Tennessee, to Urbana, Illinois, to Bozeman, Montana – now have interfaith associations, councils, and initiatives that have been started since 9/11.

Admittedly, this has not been an easy time for interreligious dialogue. Conservative Christian leaders have been emboldened to reckless statements about Islam. Jewish–Muslim dialogue initiatives have foundered with the further deterioration of peace prospects in Israel and Palestine. Islamophobia has become a staple of AM talk-radio. Basic civil rights have been undermined. And yet through all of this, dialogue initiatives have moved to a new depth of relationship. They are not only about understanding neighbors halfway around the world, but also building relationships with people who live across town or across the street.

How is it, then, that a shattered window produces a new set of relationships? How is it that an act of hatred can produce a positive echo boom of compassion? What can we all learn from these kinds of experience repeated time after time in cities and towns across America? Far from causing us to tighten our defenses and clench our fists, tragedy more often opens our hearts and creates the space for new beginnings. On one level, it seems natural, even intuitive, that this should be the case. But how can the positive echo boom of tragedy be leveraged into the creation of policy? Lessons learned at a local level were never even remotely apprehended at a national policy level. The space opened for new and powerful alliances across the world was, instead, occupied by a strategy of violent retribution, articulated in the language of war within hours of the September 11 attacks.

Women's Religious Networks has continued to meet and has involved new women in the three years since 9/11. By the time we gathered in April of 2002, the crisis of civil rights for all Americans was on the agenda. The Patriot Act had generated a new climate of fear-mongering and suspicion. The policy of reprisal was in full swing, alienating the very communities we needed as allies. Sharifa reported that people were afraid to come to the mosques, afraid to donate to Muslim charities, afraid to protest. Muslim homes and offices had been raided. Shamita Das Dasgupta told us, "September 11 became a pretext for doing what they wanted to do anyway: crack down on immigrants. Detentions, raids, targeting brown people were the order of the day. Now everyone is afraid of punitive measures."

By the time we met in May of 2003, the war in Iraq had begun, and we expanded our number to include women from other parts of the world. The war seemed predictably to be sowing dragon's teeth with each victory. Beverly Harrison, a major voice in Christian ethics, set a somber tone, now a year and a half after 9/11. "What I love most about America," she said, "is the passion for democracy, and it is that we are losing. There is a kind of fascism among us that we do not even recognize." Bold words, but words that struck a chord. Sheila Decter of the Jewish Alliance for Law and Social Action said, "It is not just the laws that have been changed, but a kind of complacency and apathy has set in. Let someone else decide. I am concerned not only about free speech, but more broadly, about civil discourse: We Americans have lost the ability to talk." Sharifa Alkhateeb observed, "There is a new demonization afoot, and the country is slipping back from basic civil liberties, from freedom of thought."

Terry Rockefeller of the September Eleventh Families for Peaceful Tomorrows brought us back to September 11 and to the hope and vision that led us to keep on talking, building bridges of words, even as we recognized the profound discouragement many of us felt. "My sister was killed in the World Trade Center," said Terry, "and I experienced, for many weeks, a tremendous collective compassion surrounding me. When I stood in line to file a victim's report, people brought coffee and hugs. When I took a taxi to the station where victims' families gathered, the taxi driver said, 'No charge.' Something happened in the world following that tragedy, and not only in America. There was a profound opening, reaching out toward America in sympathy and solidarity. And then we lost it. We need to get back to that ground of connection."

Peaceful Tomorrows is comprised of people convinced that the response to the death of their loved one should not be more violence. A few weeks earlier, they had traveled by bus from town to town all along the route between the Pentagon and Ground Zero. They had marched together through one town after another with the message "No More Victims," carrying signs "No War in Our Name." As Dr Martin Luther King Jr had put it during the Vietnam War, "The past is prophetic in that it asserts loudly that wars are poor chisels for carving out peaceful tomorrows."

Dialogue is the process of connection. There is no dialogue among religions as such. Dialogue is always among people, like the women of six religious traditions who have been part of Women's Religious Networks. Dialogue is premised not on unanimity, but on difference. Dialogue does not aim at consensus, but understanding. Dialogue does not create agreements, but it creates relationships. As Sharifa put it, "We need to build up long-term relationships – not just meetings, not just one-time encounters, but relationships of trust and knowing across religious lines."

4

Closing Chapters of Enmity

Rajmohan Gandhi

During my teens two related goals for friendship, between Hindus and Muslims and between India and Pakistan, captured my being. A role was doubtless played in this by my grandfather's life and by his death in 1948 at the hands of Hindu extremists who thought he was friendlier than necessary to Muslims and Pakistanis. From his boyhood until the last breath of his life (I was 12½ when he was killed), Mohandas Gandhi had worked for Hindu–Muslim amity.

Another factor was a recognition that despite my grandfather's teaching I harbored ill will against the neighboring country. This showed itself in 1951 when, as a 16-year-old, I heard in my New Delhi home that Liaqat Ali Khan, Prime Minister of Pakistan, had been shot at. "I hope we will hear that he is dead," I said to the man bearing the news. He froze, I was abashed at my ugly remark about someone who had done me or mine no harm, and the realization that the subcontinent was overflowing with the ill will I had entertained got me thinking.

In the decades that followed, it has been my privilege to write and work without ceasing for dialogue and reconciliation between India and Pakistan – for a day when the subcontinent can close the long chapter of enmity.

September 11 and its Aftermath

In recent years my heart has taken on an additional yearning or prayer: for a rapprochement between the West and the world of Islam. When 9/11 occurred, I was in my home just south of New Delhi, in India. My sister phoned asking me to turn the TV on, as buildings in New York, she said, had been attacked. Like the rest of the world, I spent most of the hours that followed, horrified and shocked, in front of a TV set, and my heart flew to America. As a British writer has put it, that day love flew to America from all over the world.

9/11 dried up the oceans and joined the US to the soil of the earth as a whole; America lost its safety, its separateness, its sense of being specially protected; it became one with all of vulnerable humanity. On the other hand, 9/11 also made America more fearful of the world, or at least of large sections of the world.

The War on Terrorism was America's response – an under-standable, in part unavoidable, and yet inadequate response, for it ignored the difference between a violent symptom and the cause underlying it. Reminiscent of the unsatisfying anti-communism of the cold war, the War on Terrorism, with its focus on evil men in societies declared to have failed and observing a religion declared to be flawed, discouraged an honest reflection in the USA on resentments in the Muslim world.

True, the drums of the War on Terrorism were at times accom-panied by fainter sounds of debate. "Why do they hate us?" was a question sometimes asked, if only as a formality. The answer was apparently known and obvious: they hate freedom.

"Wait a minute," some people tried to point out. "It is because they were deprived of their independence and their lands that the Arabs are angry. If the USA supports freedom for Palestine, anger toward America will turn to warmth." The argument was not heard; it got lost in a burst of shouts about dictators in Muslim lands who oppressed their people, and women in particular. Actions backed by force against perpetrators of terrorism are inescapable, but the Answer to Terrorism is a greater goal than the War on Terrorism, and the search for such an answer cannot disregard the long-standing offense caused by Israeli occupation of Arab territories, and by the USA's apparent acceptance of the occupation.

Arabs with self-respect will continue to resist the occupation, and wise Arabs will resist it in a manner that earns the support of the world community, including citizens of the USA and Israel. When innocent children, women, and men are blasted out of existence in the name of resistance, those blasts also drown out the Palestinian cry for independence.

If there is a just God, justice will come to Palestine. May it come sooner rather than later. But the Almighty is also being addressed by the loved ones of the innocent victims of suicide bombings. An answer to Israeli occupation is thus different from a war on Israeli citizens. It will call for qualities greater than what suicide bombing may require; it will need the virtues that the Qur'an greatly stresses, fortitude and patience; and it will need ingenious non-violent strategies.

In his fight against a powerful empire for India's self-respect, Gandhi understood that while violence always invited harsh reprisals on the weakest Indians, nonviolent initiatives surprised the opponent and could defeat him. I know that many Arabs often think of how Gandhi succeeded.

The West and Islam

Neither the West nor the Muslim world is a homogeneous entity. Yet the division between what is seen as the West and what is seen as the Muslim world is perhaps the most critical divide the modern world has faced.

Both sides in this divide claim to worship God and honor the value of equality. The world's Muslims insist that Islam is almost above all the religion of equality. There is God at one level, merciful and compassionate and almighty, and there is, at a lower level, humanity, where Muslims say all humans are equal, irrespective of race, or class, or gender, or nationality.

The West says the same; America says the same. All are created equal: that is America's solemn oath. It is a belief expressed at all levels. President Bush has said many times that he is certain that all are equal in the eyes of God, and that all human lives have equal value.

And yet, voices in the Islamic world portray America as Satan or a devil; and some voices in the West, including America, present Islam as a uniquely flawed religion, and Muslims as a flawed people.

Were I a Muslim, or living in a Muslim land, I would wonder at the thinking of anyone calling America satanic. This America that has offered space, opportunity, and freedom of worship to millions of Muslims from other lands, where Muslims can practice their faith and claim a share in the life of America, an America that defended the rights of the Muslims of Bosnia and Kosovo, and supported the Mujahideen of Afghanistan in their courageous struggle against Soviet rule in the 1980s – this America makes mistakes, and at times hurts the feelings of many people, but to call this America satanic is not only to utter a terrible untruth, it is also the surest way of keeping the Muslim world insulated from the progress of humankind.

And what about those who would tell America that Islam is evil? Fortunately, they are in a minority. I know of Americans who take every opportunity to underline the similarities that mark the three Abrahamic faiths; and I am aware of American scholarship that notes common elements in significant Christian and Islamic texts – for example, in Al Fateha, the opening chapter of the Qur'an, and the Lord's Prayer.

For any Christian or Jew to defame Islam is to defame siblings, some extremely cultivated and fine siblings at that. It is also hazardous. Muslims and non-Muslims live next to one another or among one another in scores of countries in varying degrees of trust and tension: in India, in Indonesia, in Bangladesh, in the Philippines, in Nigeria, in South Africa, in the Middle East, in Egypt, in Lebanon, in Cyprus, in many countries of Europe, in Russia, China, and in the USA. To spread the notion that Muslims are especially dangerous is to risk tension, division, and violence in a number of places.

But there is a deeper question here. Most Muslims are Muslims because they were born into Muslim families; most Americans are

Americans because they were born so. Blaming Muslims because they are Muslim, or Americans because they are American, means that people are being condemned for their birth, for their blood, for their heritage.

Despite all that the world has learned of the horror of condemning people for their birth, for being born to their parents; despite the horrors of the Holocaust, of slavery, of untouchability in India; we seem willing yet again to target a section of human beings for being who they are, for being Muslims or Americans.

It is true that the 9/11 attackers called themselves Muslims, and some of them may have conducted their attack in the name of Islam. Some of the killings in Rwanda in 1994 were conducted inside churches. All the killers (and the victims too) were Christians. Did that make the Rwandan killings a Christian crime? When Hindus and Buddhists are involved in terrible deeds in Sri Lanka, are we to blame Hinduism and Buddhism? Nazism and communism were enthroned, and the Holocaust carried out, in supposedly Christian lands. Are we therefore to impute a great flaw to Christianity?

Slavery was practiced, and also apartheid, in Christian societies, and often in the name of Christianity. Did the slaves blame Christianity? Were the spirituals anti-Christian? Did Nelson Mandela strive to alert his people in South Africa to an evil inherent in Christianity?

In September 2003, I saw on TV the conversation that Brit Hume of Fox News had with President Bush in the White House. In the Oval Office, Hume asked the President about the sources of his inspiration. President Bush named Lincoln and pointed to the Lincoln portrait in the room. When Hume asked how Lincoln inspired him, the President said that in a time of civil war Lincoln fought for American unity. After 9/11, the President continued, he too felt called, in the spirit of Lincoln, to invoke unity in the United States.

I think it is good to ask what Lincoln, if he were alive today, would have said. We can never know for certain, of course, yet it is perhaps useful to try. All know the timeless lines from the Second Inaugural. Referring to the two sides in the war, Lincoln said:

Both read the same Bible, and pray to the same God; and each invokes His aid against the other. It may seem strange that any men should dare ask a just God's assistance in wringing their bread from the sweat of other men's faces; but let us judge not that we be not judged.

As I look at these lines, I feel that today they speak not to two sides inside America, but to two forces appearing to clash in the world: the West, led by the USA, and the Muslim world. The challenge that Lincoln today might pose, a challenge that Martin Luther King Jr and Gandhi too might today pose, is not merely the attainment of American unity, but the healing of the larger global divide I have referred to.

After 9/11, which joined America to the suffering soil of the rest of our earth, and after the events in Iraq, Americans cannot afford to think only of uniting America, though, given today's sharp divisions in the USA, that too is a vital goal. Americans certainly can do with honest conversations with one another. Yet after 9/11 and Iraq, America and all the rest of us have to strive to heal and unite the world, and work for a just and lasting peace everywhere.

But honest questioning is also needed in Muslim and Arab lands. Surely it is time to think of new strategies against the Israeli occupation, but this deflects attention from the deep divisions inside the Muslim–Arab world, divisions that have nothing to do with Israel or the USA. Fresh thought must be given to the profound enmities that have long separated Muslim groups from one another. Where are the Muslim–Arab think tanks searching for ways in which democracy may be fostered, and the quality of life improved, in their lands? Is there enough appreciation for Arab successes in reconstruction, for example, in the renewal of recently smashed Beirut? Surely Arab pride has been bolstered by the creativity that said, "We will not use up all our energy in denouncing the enemies of Arabs. We will raise a new Beirut."

If Israeli leaders refuse to budge and Americans do not keep a sustained focus on the Palestinian question, what are the options for aggrieved Arabs and Muslims? Continuing to put appropriate pressure on Israel and the USA is certainly one, but working for visible improvements in the Muslim–Arab world is another, and the two are not necessarily in conflict.

A Final Word: Dialogue on Kashmir

As an Indian and a Hindu, I should not fail to turn the spotlight also on Hindu society and the Indian nation. I was outraged by the attacks on Muslims in Gujarat in the spring of 2002, and at the unwillingness of the state and central governments to put down or put away the attackers; and I acknowledge the fact that the discontent in Kashmir represents, among other things, a failure of Indian policies.

Yet I applaud the attempt by the former Indian Prime Minister, Atal Behari Vajpayee, for a new relationship with Pakistan and for a resolution of the Kashmir question. I am not a supporter of the party to which Mr Vajpayee belongs, and I am totally opposed to the notion of Hindu supremacy nursed by some of his influential allies; but his initiative for restoring a dialogue for normalizing India–Pakistan relations was statesmanlike. Let us hope that the current and future governments of India and Pakistan will take that dialogue forward.

5

Benjamin Franklin's Gift of Tolerance

Walter Isaacson

The great struggles of the twentieth century were against fascism and then communism. As was made clear on September 11, the great struggle of the twenty-first century will be between the forces of fanatic fundamentalism and those of tolerance.

It is important to remember that America was not born with the virtue of religious tolerance, but had to acquire it. One of the myths is that the first settlers were advocates of religious freedom. In fact, the Puritans of Boston were very intolerant, not only of witches but also of any deviation from the tribal orthodoxy. The most arcane antinomian dispute ended up forcing people to have to move and found a new state like Rhode Island.

Among those who ran away from the intolerant orthodoxy of Boston was the great American statesman Benjamin Franklin. He ended up in Philadelphia, a place unlike much of the world. There were Lutherans and Moravians and Quakers and even Jews, as well as Calvinists, living side by side in what became known as the city of brotherly love. Franklin helped formulate the creed that they would all be better off, personally and economically, if they embraced an attitude of tolerance.

Franklin believed in God and in the social usefulness of religion, but he did not subscribe to any particular sectarian doctrine. This led him to help raise money to build a new hall in Philadelphia that was, as he put it, "expressly for the use of any preacher of any religious persuasion who might desire to say something." He added: "Even if the Mufti of Constantinople were to send a missionary to preach Mohammedanism to us, he would find a pulpit at his service."

He also wrote parodies that poked fun at Puritan intolerance. In one of them, called "A Witch Trial at Mount Holly," a group of accused witches were subjected to two tests: weighed on a scale against the Bible, and tossed in the river with hands and feet bound to see if they floated. They agreed to submit – on the condition that two of the accusers take the same test. With colorful details of all the pomp, Franklin described the process. The accused and accusers all succeed in outweighing the Bible. But both the accused and one of the accusers fail to sink in the river, thus indicating that they are witches. The more intelligent spectators conclude that most people naturally float. The others are not so sure, and they resolve to wait until summer when the experiment could be tried with the subjects unclothed.

Franklin's free thinking unnerved his family. When his parents wrote of their concern over his "erroneous opinions," Franklin replied with a letter that spelled out a religious philosophy based on tolerance that would last his life. It would be vain for any person to insist that "all the doctrines he holds are true and all he rejects are false." The same could be said of the opinions of different religions as well. He had little use for the doctrinal distinctions his mother worried about. "I think vital religion has always suffered when orthodoxy is more regarded than virtue. And the Scripture assures me that at the last day we shall not be examined by what we thought, but what we did . . . that we did good to our fellow creatures. See Matthew 26." (His parents, a bit more versed in the Scripture, probably caught that he meant Matthew 25.)

Franklin believed in having the humility to be open to different opinions. That for him was not just a practical virtue, but a moral one as well. It was based on the tenet, so fundamental to most moral systems, that every individual deserves respect. During the Constitutional Convention, for example, he was willing to compromise some of his beliefs in order to play a critical role in the conciliation that produced a near-perfect document. It could

not have been accomplished if the hall had contained only cru-
saders who stood on unwavering principle. Compromisers may
not make great heroes, but they do make democracies.

By the end of his life, he had contributed to the building
funds of each and every sect in Philadelphia, including £5 for the
Congregation Mikveh Israel for its new synagogue in April 1788.
During the July 4 celebrations that year, he was too sick to leave
his bed, but the parade marched under his window. For the first
time, as per arrangements that Franklin had overseen, "the clergy
of different Christian denominations, with the rabbi of the Jews,
walked arm in arm." And when he was carried to his grave two
years later, his casket was accompanied by all the clergymen of
the city, every one of them, of every faith.

In a world that was then, as alas it still is now, bloodied by those
who seek to impose theocracies, Franklin helped to create a
new type of nation that could draw strength from its religious
pluralism. This comfort with the concept of tolerance – which was
based on an aversion to tyranny, a fealty to free expression, a willingness to compromise, the morality of respecting other individuals, and even a bit of humor and humility – is what most
distinguishes those nations and peoples that will help to create a
better and more peaceful world.

6

God's Word and World Politics

Archbishop Desmond Tutu

Frequently during our anti-apartheid struggle those who supported the apartheid government would castigate me for committing the heinous crime of mixing religion with politics. They said I was a politician trying hard to be an archbishop. Interestingly, it was those who were the privileged and who were benefiting from the unjust status quo that was being condemned who took issue with me. The oppressed, in contrast, thought I was not political enough. The privileged were enamored of their favorite dichotomies as between the sacred and the secular, the holy and the profane, the spiritual and the material.

And yet, even in a land that has enshrined constitutionally the separation of church and state, it is one of the ironies of life that politicians invest considerable resources in wooing what might be regarded as influential religious constituencies, and they are scrupulous not to upset such constituencies by advocating policies that might do that in the United States. Those calling themselves "the moral majority" have wanted to promote a particular agenda, and so political candidates have made a point of espousing causes that would endear them to such groups. Thus politicians have known that their views on abortion or gays and lesbians would likely alienate or win the favor of one or another religious group. If that is not mixing religion with politics, then I do not know what is. Those who want not do so are asking for the moon.

Religious faith and faith communities have for a long time been very significant factors in public life. Those who ignore them have usually rued their stance and lived to regret it.

The Persistence of Religious Faith of Some Sort

The fundamental distinction between religion and politics becomes clearer when we recognize the enduring characteristic of religious faith, one of the more fascinating features of human existence. Human beings are worshiping animals. It is almost as universal and as inescapable as breathing. Part of our makeup is that we must worship something or someone. It appears we are created for the transcendent, for that which is other than we are, conceived as higher, better, more intelligent, more powerful, evoking reverence of some sort, and this tends to drive us onto our knees. It is healthy when this other is truly transcendent, holy, and good, the one whom most designate as God or the divine. There are those who have refused to worship this one, but worship they must. They may bend their knee to something less than God, perhaps to success, ambition, or sex, and almost always they are disillusioned as their God turns into dust and ashes. We are by nature religious – which does not tell us what it is that we worship, or what sort of persons our worship has helped us to become.

Religious faith is resilient and not easily destroyed. Many atheistic regimes have learned to their cost that religious faith is not easy to get rid of. Frequently, the more a religion is persecuted and proscribed, the more it seems to flourish and grow. The Soviet Communist regime tried its utmost to destroy the Russian Orthodox Church and other faith communities. Try as hard as it might, eventually it had to concede defeat because, despite all the disadvantages heaped on it as a forbidden thing, frustratingly from the atheistic government's perspective, the persecuted faiths have flourished. That seems to be the case in other places as well, such as China and elsewhere.

Religion is a potent force, but it is in fact morally neutral. It is automatically neither good nor bad. It can be either, depending on what it inspires its adherent to do. It was religious zeal that drove Martin Luther King Jr to struggle for justice and equity in the American Civil Rights Movement. It was her faith that inspired Mother Teresa to expend herself so prodigally on behalf of the derelicts and the discarded of Calcutta. It is his faith that has sustained the Dalai Lama in the many years of exile from his beloved Tibet, enabling him to be one of the holiest, most serene persons I have been privileged to meet. But religion has had a malignant impact in many other situations. Those who have killed doctors who procured abortions believed they were carrying out a religious duty. Christians went on Crusades to drive out the infidels from the Holy Land. Wars have flared up between adherents of the same faith in many wars of religion that were for long a prominent feature of Europe, something that, sadly, has not disappeared completely, as the sectarian strife in Northern Ireland shows, where Christian is pitted against fellow Christian. In Iraq the parlous situation has been exacerbated by rivalry between Sunni and Shia Muslims.

Thus religion has the capacity to produce saints or rogues, perpetrators of the most vile atrocities. It really depends on what the adherent allows the religion to accomplish in him or her. This is a very important assertion, especially in our fraught days when we speak so facilely of the war between civilizations and characterize the ghastly violence of fanatics as something somehow inherent in the faith they claim to espouse, and so we slide so easily into stereotyping. Because some, perhaps many, of those who are called terrorists are Muslims, we quickly find ourselves thinking of Islam as a violent faith that eggs on its adherents to engage in acts of terror. We end up suspecting all Arabs, and then it is soon people of Middle Eastern descent, and then any swarthy person or any stranger as we feed our growing xenophobia. Thus it was a huge shock to many Westerners when they discovered that the Bosnian Muslims looked exactly like themselves ethnically and not as they had always believed Muslims should look. It is a great tragedy when a whole religion is tarred with the same brush as that appropriate for extremist adherents of Islam. Christians would bristle with justified resentment if their faith was vilified by being identified with the fundamentalists who believe they are doing God's will in killing doctors who help women by procuring abortions, or those others whose homophobia has led them to string up a gay man on a fence leaving him to die an excruciating death, or those such as the Ku Klux Klan who believe their vile racism to be sanctioned by the Scriptures and are not ashamed to use as their particular trademark something that dishonors a symbol that Christians revere deeply, a flaming Cross, when they have lynched a black man or torched his home or place of worship. We would be appalled that anyone could ever imagine that these fringe groups represented mainstream Christianity.

We should be categorical and quite unequivocal. There is no war between people of different faiths because of that difference of faith *per se*. There is no war between Islam and Christianity or between Islam and Judaism. There are adherents of different faiths who engage in all kinds of nefarious activities, including violence and terrorism. The Oklahoma bombers were Caucasian and Christian, but that did not make Christianity a violent religion that encouraged its adherents to engage in acts of terrorism. Terrorists happen sometimes to be Christian, sometimes Muslim, sometimes Jewish, etc. The cause of terrorism lies not in their faith but in various circumstances: injustice, oppression, poverty, disease, hunger, ignorance, and so on. To combat this terrorism, we should not foolishly speak of "crusades" against this or that faith, but we should eradicate the root causes that can drive people to the desperation that compels them to engage in desperate acts. We will not win the war against terrorism until we do that.

The Worth of Faiths

The influence of faiths is not only malign and baneful. Wonderfully, it is what has been responsible for some of the most spectacular achievements of humankind. We have seen some quite awful things; Christians need to be among the most modest because of the many ghastly things that Christians have perpetrated. We cannot be hoity-toity and speak disdainfully of "those terrorists," many of whom have been non-Christians. After all, devout Christians were among the most notorious slave owners, saw no contradiction between their faith and their ownership of fellow human beings, often fellow Christians, as if they were mere chattel and beasts of burden. It was Christians who gave the world the horror of the Holocaust in Nazi Germany and the excesses of fascism in Italy and Franco's Spain. It was not pagans, but Christians, who found alleged biblical justifications for the injustice and inhumanity of apartheid in South Africa. It was a Christian leader who ordered nuclear weapons of mass destruction to be dropped on Hiroshima and Nagasaki on innocent unarmed civilians. It has been Christians at one another's throats in Northern Ireland. The Rwandan genocide happened in a land almost exclusively Christian. We Christians have much that should make us hang our heads in shame. But there is much in our faith and in that of others for which we can be deeply thankful.

Many faiths have a very high doctrine of human beings, including the Judaeo-Christian faiths claiming that human beings are made in God's image and with a worth that is intrinsic and universal. It does not depend on extrinsic things such as ethnicity, gender, status, and so on, and it is possessed by all, regardless. The *imago Dei* is the basis of the Universal Declaration of Human Rights and is the reason the world stood as one in its condemnation of apartheid and all racism. The word of God unequivocally affected the world of politics; it was wonderful to behold the cooperation between the various faith communities in their opposition to apartheid. We walked arm in arm with Muslims, Hindus, Jews, and others on our protest demonstrations against the scourge of apartheid.

Virtually all the faiths teach fundamental moral values shared by all: honesty, fidelity in marriage, truthfulness, courage, compassion, concern for the other, the unity of humankind as one family, and peace. No religion teaches that it is good to steal, to lie, to be abusive of others, to kill. They all in different ways extol peace. These are values or ideals that world politics should strive after. These are the values to inform the world of politics.

Many of the faiths exhort their adherents to be caring stewards of the rest of creation. Ecological concerns are a deeply religious, spiritual matter. To pollute the environment, to be responsible for the disastrous warming, is not just wrong and should be a criminal offense, but it is certainly morally wrong. It is a sin.

Faiths teach that we are ultimately a family, and our destiny as the human family is in our hands as a common destiny. It is to be at odds with the precepts of most religions to be indifferent to the suffering and misery of others, to watch unconcerned when others are hungry and poor, assailed by disease and ignorance when there is much that the affluent of all faiths could do to alleviate their lot. It is obscene to spend as much as we do on arms, on budgets of death and destruction, when, as we so well know, a small fraction of those budgets would ensure that our sisters and brothers everywhere, God's children, members of our family, would have clean water, enough to eat, an adequate education and health care, and a decent home. We can do it if we allow our faiths to inspire us.

All faiths teach that this is a moral universe. Evil, injustice, and oppression can never have the last word. Right, goodness, love, laughter, caring, sharing and compassion, peace and reconciliation, will prevail over their ghastly counterparts. The powerful unjust ones who throw their weight about, who think that might is right, will bite the dust and get their comeuppance. Those who rule, those who engage in politics, must know this, and they must know that power is for service, not self-aggrandizement; power is for the sake of the ruled.

Conclusion

The policies that the United Nations espouses – development rather than conflict and war, the eradication of poverty, the advancement of the cause of children and women, the striving after justice and respect for the human rights for all, freedom and democracy – all these are not only sanctioned by the holy scriptures of most faiths, but have the divine approval of God's blessing. Outside the UN building is a monument that bears the inscription, "to beat our swords into ploughshares and our spears into pruning hooks." Such work of promoting global peace and harmony is a high calling, a deeply spiritual vocation. It is God's work.

This essay is based on a lecture by Archbishop Tutu delivered at the United Nations on March 17, 2004. Original lecture copyrighted by Desmond Tutu. Used with permission. All rights reserved.

Part III

Pathways to Dialogue and Understanding

7

The Role of the Media in Promoting Tolerance

Shashi Tharoor

At the beginning of September 2002, I was in a television studio in North Carolina, in the southern United States, for an interview about the UN. While waiting to go on air, I was told about the TV show the station was proudly about to broadcast the following day. Called "The Rise and Fall of Jim Crow," it was a searing documentary series about the oppression of blacks in the American South, featuring archival material, photographs, and interviews with black and white Americans who had lived through the period of racial discrimination and segregation. "We cannot understand why we continue to have racial difficulties," said the director, Richard Wormser, "without understanding this period of our history. It is part of my legacy as a white person, as it is part of the legacy of black people."

What is striking is that this series was to be broadcast in a state where the memory of blacks being denied the vote, refused service at white-owned restaurants, forced to sit in separate seats on buses and trains, and not allowed the same educational opportunities as whites, is still relatively fresh in the minds of middle-aged Southerners of both races. Now television was helping both blacks and whites to confront the past in order to better understand the present. And North Carolina's schools were embracing the TV show by incorporating it into their social studies curriculums and encouraging students to embark on their own oral history projects.

This was an excellent example of the way in which the media today can, and sometimes do, work to promote understanding and tolerance across the racial or ethnic divide. But the media can also do the opposite. In the wrong hands, or with the wrong motives, it is a tool to incite hatred and violence. In Afghanistan under the Taliban, where women were denied the chance to read, and where all were denied access to alternative sources of information, the media's promotion of the creed of the Qur'an and the Kalashnikov (the Qur'an crudely interpreted, the Kalashnikov crudely made) had devastating consequences for societal well-being and human rights. In Rwanda in 1994, "Radio Milles Collines" played a chilling role in the fomenting of prejudice, fear, and greed, with a devastating outcome: the genocidal slaughter of 800,000 people. And who can forget the hatred and lies spewed by radio and TV stations of all stripes during the wars and ethnic murders that tormented the former Yugoslavia?

But "hate media," universally detested, is fortunately an aberration. In most countries, the press enjoys a degree of freedom, and that includes the freedom to do good as well as harm. It is not my intention, as a United Nations official, to prescribe a particular role for the media. On the contrary, an independent media by definition should say and print what it thinks fit, without interference of any kind, a right enshrined in Article 19 of the Universal Declaration of Human Rights. An independent, impartial media is one of the quintessential building blocks of democracy. Freedom of the press is the mortar that binds together the bricks of freedom, and it is also the open window embedded in those bricks. By giving voice and visibility to all people – and especially the poor, the marginalized, and the minorities – the media can help remedy the inequalities, the corruption, the ethnic tensions, and the human rights abuses that form the root causes of many conflicts.

As the senior United Nations official charged with working with the world media to advance the goals and aspirations of the organization, I am all too aware of the complexity of the tasks facing my colleagues and myself. We cannot afford the luxury of a "message of the day," because each day we are simultaneously putting out several dozen messages everywhere. We deal with a global audience that is both vast and fragmented, whose interests and passions diverge across borders. We try to rouse concern amongst the rich and the tranquil about the plight of the poor and the strife-torn. We seek to overcome the indifference of the information-saturated while trying not to neglect the needs of the information-starved. We respond to the demands of the sophisticated media of the developed North while trying not to overlook or alienate the media of the developing South. We have to work with journalists and advocates on both sides of every dispute. And we do all this in an uneven global environment, which offers opportunities and pitfalls for us all.

In one sense, globalization, whatever its sins and limitations, plays a positive role. The media bring glimpses of events from every corner of the globe to our breakfast tables, our living rooms, and, increasingly, to our computers and our mobile phones. Any doubt I might have had about the reach and influence of global mass communications was dispelled when I happened to be in St Petersburg, Russia, for a conference and was approached by a Tibetan Buddhist monk in his robes, thumping a cymbal and chanting, who paused to say "I've seen you on BBC!" New communications technology has shrunk the world, and in a real sense made it all one. In many ways the information revolution has changed the world for the better, by providing a window that allows for the possibility that people everywhere will better understand their neighbors, and by allowing people who once would not even have known about the possibilities the world has to offer a means to take up those offers.

But the information revolution, unlike the French Revolution, is at present one with much *liberté*, some *fraternité*, and no *égalité*. And its twin, globalization, has yet to deliver the goods, or even the tools to obtain them, to many in great need. The 400,000 citizens of Luxembourg have access to more internet bandwidth than Africa's 760 million citizens. The dividing line between North and South is not just the poverty line but the fibre-optic and high-speed digital lines. If "digital divide" is a cliché of our time, it represents a reality that cannot be denied.

The media are not exempt from the consequences of this divide. While globalization gives us greater opportunities to understand the world around us, the mass media still reflect principally the interests of its producers. What passes for international culture is usually the culture of the economically developed world. There is the occasional Third World voice, but it speaks a First World language. As far back as Congo in 1962, the journalist Edward Behr saw a TV newsman in the camp of violated Belgian nuns calling out: "Anyone here been raped and speak English?" It was not enough to have suffered; one must have suffered and be able to convey one's suffering in the language of the journalist. Are those speaking for their cultures in the globalized media the most authentic representatives of them?

The reality of globalization was also made starkly clear on September 11, 2001. After 9/11 there can be no easy retreat into isolationism, no comfort in the illusion that the problems of the rest of the world need not trouble the fortunate few. The world now understands another cliché, that of the global village, because a fire that starts in a remote thatched hut or dusty tent in one corner of that village can melt the steel girders of the tallest skyscrapers in the opposite corner of the global village.

And yet the response to terrorism sometimes seems likely to undermine the very institutions of pluralism and tolerance that offer the best alternative to fanatics and killers. The media have a vital role to play in monitoring the efforts of governments to effectively combat and prevent terrorist attacks without simultaneously eroding the human rights of innocent citizens and migrants. UN Secretary-General Kofi Annan has often echoed the observation that those who are willing to give up liberty for security will end up with neither security nor liberty. During the year after 9/11, as an increase in hate crimes against brown-skinned minorities in the West was widely noted, there was concern that the issue was being neglected in the mainstream media. The International Council on Human Rights Policy charged in 2002 that the Western media had not done an adequate job in reporting on such hate crimes in Europe or North America. Ironically, when I addressed the South Asian Journalists' Association in New York a few days after September 11, 2001, the convenor asked the largely Indian and Pakistani audience whether they had encountered any recent discrimination because of their appearance. Practically every hand in the room shot up.

But I have also been impressed by the way the respectable Western press has made real efforts to avoid falling simplistically into a Huntingtonian paradigm that treats all of Islamic civilization as one undifferentiated terrorist threat. I am impressed by the fact that newspapers in Europe and America, and to a lesser degree television stations, have devoted more space to the problems of Islamic countries and have assigned more correspondents to the Muslim world than previously. This is vital, because we all must know each other better if we are to understand each other.

The media need to recognize that civilizations are not monoliths; each human civilization has a great deal of diversity within it. Religion and culture are merely amongst the many variables governing the actions and policies of states. States with a religion in common often have other differences amongst them; we just have to consider the contrasting positions taken by different Islamic states over the Taliban rule over Afghanistan to illustrate the point. Indeed, many of today's intercultural conflicts are a result of perceived cultural humiliation. Much of what is happening in parts of the Islamic world, simplistically described as "fundamentalism," is an assertion of cultural identities that have been allowed to feel marginalized or thwarted. The answer lies clearly in cultural diversity, and in the development of democracy at local, national, and international levels to provide a context for pluralism to thrive. The media are key in conveying the message that it is ultimately diversity that gives the human species its splendor, and diversity has facilitated progress through learning from our different experiences. Every time we fail to respect each other's right to different beliefs and religious expression, and ways of life, our humanity is diminished.

It is only by perpetuating the blind hatred of strangers, of an "Other," that terrorism can flourish. Such hatred is in turn the product of three factors: fear, rage, and incomprehension – fear of what the Other might do to you, rage at what you believe the Other has done to you, and incomprehension about who or what the Other really is. If terrorism is to be tackled and ended, we will have to deal with each of these three factors by attacking the igno-rance that sustains them. We will have to know each other better, learn to see ourselves as others see us, learn to recognize hatred and deal with its causes, learn to dispel fear, and above all just learn about each other. We cannot do any of this without the media.

Secretary-General Kofi Annan once suggested that the media consider practicing "preventive journalism" – along the lines of the concept of "preventive diplomacy" – reporting on potential crises before they erupt, so that the spotlight of the media might prevent an eruption, or mobilize international action before lives are lost. He has not returned to this theme, in part because he does not feel it appropriate to tell the media how they should cover events. But it would be helpful if the media continue to search beyond the headlines, to give attention to conflicts and crises at an early stage, in order to assist and encourage an early response.

The media, along with human rights NGOs, play a vital role in providing early warning of human rights abuses, and help mobilize political will to galvanize the international community to take action. The UN itself has developed considerable experi-ence of working with the media in promoting reconciliation in divided societies, particularly as part of UN peacekeeping and peace-building operations. The media can also help frame issues in ways that diplomats, trying to bring both sides of a con-flict together, cannot. Thus in the Balkans it was the media that gave currency to the odious term "ethnic cleansing" and helped generate sympathy and public pressure for its international denunciation.

Much of the developed world's population obtains its news from television, where the motto is all too often: "If it bleeds, it leads." Television is better at conveying image than context. In the process the search for news, for a good "story," often becomes an end in itself, divorced from the human needs of its subjects. Jour-nalism, that most essential of professions, is also the most preda-tory; it feeds on suffering, on misfortune, on injustice, all of which it seeks to depict rather than to redress. And yet, without it, no real change would be possible, since change requires awareness, the real stock-in-trade of the journalist. In our increasingly inter-dependent world, it is no longer possible to shelter behind claims of ignorance of foreign lands; news about anywhere is available to even the most incurious, in papers, on TV, and most of all on the internet. What happens anywhere in our globalizing world increasingly affects us all. As someone once said about water pollution, we all live downstream.

And so it is particularly important after September 11th that we take a deeper look, a look beyond violence, at the causes of violence, and beyond apparent clashes between civilizations toward commonality and dialogue among civilizations. As Socrates taught us, "There is only one good, knowledge, and only one evil, ignorance." By depicting and promoting that vital exchange of ideas and information regardless of frontiers, the media can play their part to make possible a global civilization defined by its tolerance of dissent, its celebration of cultural diversity, and its insistence on fundamental, universal human rights.

Earlier in this essay I disavowed any intention of being prescriptive to the media. Yet, it is hard not to wish that the media devote more time to minorities, their plight and their problems, and to bringing the horrors of racism and religious fundamentalism of all kinds to light. The media can hire more journalists and editors from minorities, and can carry out educational campaigns with an anti-racism message. Intolerance can be solved not through censorship, but through an ever-livelier debate in which the ideas of the hatemongers can be defeated. The media must provide space for such a debate to take place.

At the global level, the media must recognize that there exist around us many societies whose richness lies in their soul and not in their soil, whose past may offer more wealth than their present, whose culture is more valuable than their technology. Recognizing that this might be the case and affirming that cultural distinctiveness is as central to humanity's sense of its own worth as the ability to eat, drink, and sleep under a roof is part of the challenge before the media today.

The only way to ensure that this challenge is met is to preserve cultural freedom in all societies, to guarantee that individual voices find expression, that all ideas and forms of art are enabled to flourish and contend for their place in the sun. We heard nearly a century ago that the world must be made safe for democracy. That goal is vital, and it is increasingly being realized. But it will not be fulfilled unless we also realize that it is now time for all of us to work to make the world safe for diversity.

8

Civilization, Human Rights, and Collective Responsibility

Sergio Vieira de Mello

If we are to discuss world civilization, whatever that may mean, it is important that we remember those who have suffered as a result of a breakdown of civilization. We must also pay tribute to the women, men, and children who continue to suffer the impact of armed conflict. By conservative estimates, some 8 million men, women, and children died in the Great War, the war, I need hardly add, that was supposed to end all wars. Countless others were wounded, imprisoned, displaced, or disappeared. Millions more were scarred by this horror, a horror that occurred among what are viewed as being some of the preeminent civilizations of that time.

The international community resolved, at the end of the War, to never again allow such human devastation. How wrong could they be? Governments banded together to establish the League of Nations, an organization dedicated to promoting international cooperation and achieving peace and security. Many consider the League to have been unsuccessful. They consider it so because it failed to prevent the outbreak of the Second World War, which was a conflict – to the extent these comparisons have any meaning – still more terrible than the First.

Yet it remains a fact that its creation did see the emergence of a deeper appreciation and awareness of human dignity and the sanctity of human life, as well as of the world's growing inter-connectedness. It laid the foundation for the establishment of the United Nations and paved the way for the international protection of human rights. It is a source of pride to me that the office I arrived at when I took the job as United Nations High Commissioner for Human Rights in 2002 is called the "Palais Wilson," the original home of the League of Nations.

"Wilsonianism" is a concept that is frequently derided as being either naive or a failure, or both; I disagree entirely with the former and only partially with the latter. It would be wrong to underestimate the importance of valuing these post-war achievements. It would be difficult to imagine the establishment today of a similar framework for attempting to ensure peace, security, and respect for human rights, such as the UN system, if these institutions did not already exist. That really is a question to ponder, and one I will not attempt an answer: Would the world we live in today have the capacity and the vision to create a United Nations as pure in its ideals as the one established in 1945? What would the world look like today had the United Nations not existed?

It is fortunate that we do not have to answer these questions for real. In the post-war years the international community committed to a set of basic universal values: equality, dignity, tolerance, and non-discrimination. We recognized, through the Universal Declaration of Human Rights, that "the inherent dignity and the equal and inalienable rights of all members of the human family is the foundation of freedom, justice and peace in the world." Freedom from fear and want were our common aspirations.

And we agreed, in words of truly elemental passion and force, that "we the peoples" would be "determined to save succeeding generations from the scourge of war." Together, we created a set of international human rights standards rooted firmly in these values and goals. Yet we have failed in our duties to ensure that these standards are upheld. Too often our world excludes and marginalizes those who, as a result of violence, inequality, intolerance, or discrimination are incapable of participating in any meaningful way, and worse: who have misery upon misery heaped upon them.

What is Civilization?

These observations lead me to the conclusion that civilization is a concept that eludes definition. This is a problem in terms of academic rigor, for I use the word "civilization" often in this essay; but a definition risks being either pretentious or subjective or incomplete, or a combination of these failings. And I am even more skeptical of attempting a definition of "world civilization," which has alarming connotations of pan-uniformity. The best I can do is to suggest, first, that we should eschew homogeneity and embrace difference, and, second, that focusing on common perceptions of human dignity may be more fruitful than the pursuit of one world civilization.

The difficulty of obtaining a satisfactory definition should not be allowed to obfuscate the picture. I know what is uncivilized; I have seen it. We all know. In my work with the United Nations, most of which I have spent in what we in peaceful and prosperous countries refer to euphemistically as "the field," I have seen the best and the worst of what we have to offer each other. Such behavior can be found everywhere.

As a UN worker I have had to pause and wonder how different societies can develop such ruthless disregard for human life. Common perceptions of "civilization" have largely positive connotations. They suggest both a moral milieu as well as the attainment of some sort of cultural summit: they evoke images of arts and culture, enlightenment and sophistication. They suggest evolution in a non-biological sense, progress in *social* development.

But I would suggest that the term "civilization" risks, but by no means implicitly carries, worryingly negative notions. These are notions of cultural superiority, elitism, imperialism, and Western idealism. If one considers oneself civilized, after all, then those who are different are *un*civilized.

Indeed, it was only a few years ago that it was suggested that Western concepts were so dominant, so incontrovertibly accepted, that what we were witnessing was an "end of history" in the sense that there was no longer the fuel for a clash of civilizations. Who would really dare propound such hubristic notions now? Lest we forget, the word "civilization" has been used throughout the course of history to justify brutality, expansionist thinking and behavior, colonialism, even slavery and genocide, as in my continent, the Americas. In carrying out these acts, these civilizations argued that they were, in fact, on "civilizing" missions. Our discussion of world civilization must bear these facts in mind. Some might argue that at the start of this new millennium we have achieved world civilization – that is, an advanced stage of social development at the global level, a contemporary version, so to speak, of Hegel's *Weltgeist*, the spirit of the world. It is true that we live in an era of unprecedented wealth and extraordinary technological, scientific, and educational advancement. The world is more democratic today than ever before: 140 countries now hold multi-party elections. The number of inter-state wars, and of the human lives lost as a result of those wars, has dropped considerably.

Globalization, Poverty, and Collective Apathy

Global markets have opened up as the result of new technology, and increased economic integration has helped to create new opportunities. Globalization has created the potential for greater communication and exchanges between different cultures. In so doing it has paved the way for greater human freedom. But in spite of these many positive developments, the end of the cold war – now often treated almost with nostalgia by some – and the continuing process of globalization have also given rise to many uncertainties.

New forms of terrorism have emerged, creating untold suffering recently in New York, in Bali, and in Moscow. The human costs of terrorism have been felt equally in the Philippines, the Middle East, Algeria, and Sri Lanka, just as they have been felt – in years now thankfully receding – in many countries of Western Europe. Internal armed conflicts continue to ravage countries around the world.

Seemingly intractable global conditions – poverty, HIV/AIDS, racism, and gender inequality – continue to cause widespread human misery. These conditions contribute to the growing mar-

ginalization of individuals and communities and, where left un-
addressed, create tensions, jeopardize human development, and
threaten security. Each of these constitutes the antithesis of
civilization. Although international wars have decreased in number, internal conflicts have killed about 3.6 million people over the last
decade. Particularly worrisome is the increasing victimization of
civilians: more than 90 percent of those injured or killed in
post–cold war conflicts have been civilians, and half of these were
children. The number of refugees and internally displaced people
has risen sharply, an indication of both the increased intensity of
today's conflicts and disregard for the non-combatant.

The situation is worsening: the resurgence of anti-Semitism,
including in Western Europe, as well as the rise of the new and
disturbing phenomenon of vilifying Islam, are particularly worrying and, alone, pose serious questions to any defenders there may
be of the concept of a world civilization. Intolerance, as one of its
many evils, is rarely honest about its motives; it hides behind many
pretexts.

Protecting human rights is first and foremost the responsibility
of states. Yet governments have been too passive in tackling different recent manifestations of intolerance and, in fact, often contribute to them.

Many of the profound political, social, and economic changes
that have characterized the past decade or so have impacted negatively on women. The traumatic effects on women of conflict and
human displacement are exacerbated by sexual violence. Economic instability and change hamper progress in the achievement
of gender equality, notably due to the feminization of poverty.
Institutional discrimination against women – in particular, occu-
pational discrimination and segregation – along with negative
gender stereotypes persist in virtually all societies.

This situation is absurd, not just because of the denial of fundamental rights it entails for women, but also because of the
untapped advantages for us all that we are denied. Women are a
force for peace. They are invariably the glue that binds families
and communities; they are the reconcilers. They are economic
providers and, in many places, they are in the majority. To have

them effectively silenced – to have women not participating fully in the shaping of their societies – makes no sense.

These problems are not fundamentally new. Human beings have lived with war, disease, and inequality for centuries. What is different today is that we have no excuse to be unaware of the divide between the world's rich and poor, the powerful and powerless, the included and marginalized. We cannot today justify claiming ignorance of the cost that this divide imposes on the poor and dispossessed while at the same time claiming that we are civilized.

There is, or so it can seem, a palpable lack of empathy toward those affected: a dulling of critical analysis of policies that impact communities and societies outside and beyond our own. But more than that, I suspect there is a dulling of our ability to appreciate what this impact may mean, in real terms, on those affected. The danger in assuming that we, the so-called international community, are "civilized" is this collective apathy to which we have become accustomed.

The Universality of Human Rights

This cannot continue. We can no longer act as if what happens in our immediate communities is all that matters, as if we owe solidarity only to those within our neighborhood, city, or country. We should nurture our sense of self as part of a common humanity. We should appreciate better the ways in which we can all benefit from cooperation and solidarity across lines of nationality, gender, race, and economic status. We should seize the potential of globalization to become a unifying and inclusive force: a globalization that places the promotion and protection of human rights at the heart of its objectives and strategies.

Human rights do indeed have a critical role to play today. Their indivisibility and universality are perhaps the closest concepts we have to being the foundations of a civilized world, as opposed to a world civilization. The principles of social, political, and economic inclusion are essentially based on rights and responsibilities. Those in positions of power and privilege, however, too often see rights and responsibilities as a threat to their own interests. As a set of universally accepted values, principles, and standards, which apply equally to all people, human rights should in fact be seen as a tool to help build stable and prosperous communities.

Helping to foster the rule of law will be the overarching theme of my work as High Commissioner. The rule of law is the linchpin of human rights protection; without it, respect for our dignity and for the equality and security of all human beings is meaningless. Human rights work, in other words, is not just about morals or politics, but about responsibilities, legal obligations, and accountability. Through the framework of the rule of law, human rights provide individuals with recourse when decisions are made that may adversely affect them. They also provide a means by which to attempt to ensure that those adverse decisions or actions are not taken in the first place.

Rights aim to empower individuals by allowing us to use them as leverage for action. They legitimize our voices, placing emphasis on the participation of individuals in decision making. They seek to avoid discrimination through their equal application to us all.

Effective human development can be achieved only where people are free to participate in the decisions that shape their lives. The free will of people to determine their own political, economic, social, and cultural systems, and their full participation in all aspects of their lives, is, to me, axiomatic. It is, in short, inherently "civilizing."

Democratic governance is based on the extension of civil and political rights: in particular, the right to participate in political life. It is a basic form of organization or political order whose underlying principle is a recognition of the equal dignity and worth of every human being. Democracy provides the most appropriate framework for the realization of human rights. By allowing a voice in political decisions, it is instrumental in enabling us to realize other rights.

I do not suggest that democracy is the solution to all problems. It is vital to recognize and address democracy's shortcomings: it does not automatically correlate with respect for human rights, nor does its presence necessarily lead to economic and social development. The vast majority of democratic countries still limit important civil and political rights, and many often neglect economic and social rights, partly because this neglect is less obvious and does not hurt the electoral outcomes for those in power.

Countries in transition face particular challenges, as the replacement of an authoritarian regime with an electoral system does not solve human rights problems. On the contrary, the transition to a new order often brings to the surface a complex web of human rights issues. Just look at the challenges that were faced by South Africa, and that are faced today by East Timor, Sierra Leone, and Afghanistan, in figuring out how best to acknowledge the abuses of their recent pasts, break the cycle of impunity, and ensure that violence does not recur.

Democracy faces other weaknesses as well. It has been described as little more than giving an individual a choice on one day in every four years or so. It has been described also as amounting to tyranny of the majority. The majority may trample on the rights of minorities in many ways: by excluding their participation, manipulating the media and political rights, setting aside the rule of law at the expense of minority rights in times of social upheaval, repressing minority cultural practices, language, and religion, and overriding minority economic interests all in pursuit of interests of the majority. Such utilitarianism often sneaks inside democracies; we should be alert to the risk.

At the same time, we should not ignore the many societies in which majorities are marginalized by minorities. Consider particularly women, youths, and the least privileged. It is still overly simplistic to assert that full respect for human rights, democracy, and the rule of law can prevent a meltdown of society. A civic order based on respect for human rights suggests that the authorities will respect individual rights. Governments have the primary responsibility for the protection and promotion of human rights, but civic order also requires that the members of that polity, the citizens, take on board their responsibilities towards each other.

Corporate Citizenship and Globalism from Below

This brings me to reflect on a relatively new concept of citizenship: the concept of corporate citizenship. If citizenship is defined as the rights and duties of a member of a country, then companies, by extension, share those same rights and duties. The citizenship performance of corporations varies just as for countries; both represent the interests of individuals.

In 2000, United Nations Secretary-General Kofi Annan launched the Global Compact. In the very first principle, he asked companies to support and respect the protection of international human rights within their sphere of influence. The citizenship performance of companies in this realm varies, as we know; but thinking about the meaning of citizenship forces us all to consider the extent of our obligations and how best to meet them.

I come from a country famous for its rich cultural diversity. It is a country that has pursued policies of development over decades and even centuries that have, let us face it, impinged upon and marginalized its original indigenous inhabitants. If we look at recent years, we can say with some honesty that corporate Brazil – and I include international companies – has been one of the principal sources of the destruction not only of the forest itself but of the indigenous peoples' livelihoods and communities. Brazil has made striking material advances, but they have come at a price: indigenous peoples have often been victims rather than beneficiaries of these changes.

For indigenous peoples, the corporate sector presents such a new challenge with its technology, its apparently unlimited wealth, and its legal expertise. It is not easy to find the balance that will protect indigenous peoples' rights, ensure the legitimate obligations of governments toward all their citizens, and not impede entrepreneurship and development. Some requirements are clear, however. Fair rules are important. Benefit sharing is vital. The prior informed consent of the affected communities is an ideal toward which we should be aiming. My idea of civilization is one that includes indigenous peoples and their diverse cultures.

Corporate and government responsibilities are converging in another way as well. While corporations are, through the conceptual framework of citizenship, being cast as world actors with specific responsibilities commensurate with their influence, at the same time individuals are increasingly voicing global rather than local concerns. There is recognition that we are part of a global community in which our actions impact life in other regions and that the concerns of others are also our concerns. While they may not always necessitate global solutions, these worldwide connections across frontiers are generating a sense of responsibility, not only within one's community but also within empathetic networks across the world. This kind of interest and participation, what has been called "globalization from below," is vital to a healthy world civilization. This manifestation of globalization provides some cause for optimism.

Toward a Higher Civilization

We may be overreaching and misleading ourselves to talk of world civilization. More important than striving to attain a "civilized" state, if indeed such a state is definable, is the need to focus on, highlight, and better appreciate the universality of human dignity. That, to me, would be a more productive avenue of investigation.

Human rights provide the best road map for this investigation. The principles of the UN Charter, the Universal Declaration, and the other human rights instruments adopted in the last half-century are the closest we have to a universal code of conduct. These instruments provide the necessary building blocks to ensure that our common humanity is an inclusive one, built on values such as tolerance and dignity. The commitments they embody have been accepted voluntarily. It is the responsibility of all to ensure that they are respected.

Human rights possess a number of additional advantages of which we should be aware. First, they are easy to understand. Yet we have a tendency to engage in lengthy rarefied debates defining this right or that. Indeed, we do too much of this. The results are often confusion, a degree of acrimony, and failure to implement the right in question. The victims, needless to say, have no problem in understanding what right it is that is being violated and how. Definitions and semantics do have their role to play.

Second, human rights can provide foils for our failure to move forward. With rights come attendant responsibilities. States and non-governmental institutions alike must live up to their responsibilities to ensure the respect for human rights. Human rights apply to everyone. Inherent within them is a celebration of their universality and diversity. Ensuring that we allow for such diversity, and, by so doing, ensuring that we respect human rights, is my main message.

Ensuring that we allow for different cultures and people to coexist and flourish alongside one another is as important a priority today as ever. There is, ironically, a unity in this. The task before us is to find the great truth of this unity, to transcend the repetitions and contradictions of our earthly experience and discover the unity of the world. This may be what civilization is all about.

9

Endless Enemies or Human Security

Jody Williams

With the fall of the Soviet Union, many felt a moment of euphoria at the possibilities of a changed world. People hoped that with the globe no longer divided into two warring camps – warring rhetorically and, in some cases, literally – standing armies and military budgets might be reduced. The euphoric vision saw these reductions, perhaps accompanied by a dramatic decrease in the global arms trade, resulting in a "peace dividend," the resources of which would be applied to resolving some of the intractable problems facing humankind.

Others took a much more sober view, recognizing that without a deliberate and concerted effort to take a new approach to a changed and changing world, not much would really be different. While the sole remaining superpower would no longer have to worry itself with the Communist menace, some felt concern about how it would react in the newly unipolar world. Many speculated that it would begin to seek other global enemies, in part because real threats continue to exist, but also in order to justify continued militarism as the country contemplated how to react to its unique position as the military, economic, and technological giant in the post-cold war world.

Almost before meaningful dialogue about that new world could even be considered, Iraq invaded Kuwait, and the 1991 Gulf War ensued. I remember wondering at that time if that conflict would mark an attempt to demonize Arabic peoples or those of Muslim faith, whether there was a new "enemy" in the making. There was some hope that this would not be the case when the Gulf War was limited to pushing Iraqi forces out of Kuwait, and not the overthrow of Saddam Hussein and the occupation of Iraq. Not long after that war, a new administration came to power in Washington that put serious effort into resolving the Israel/ Palestine question and continued to fuel hopes for significant changes in the post-cold war world.

It was in this now seemingly brief window of high expectations that some bold new initiatives were created that provided collective solutions to various problems of global scope. One of those initiatives was the global movement to ban anti-personnel landmines, important not only because it led to an international treaty which for the first time in history eliminated a conventional weapon that had been used by nearly all fighting forces for about 100 years, but also because it provided a successful model of government–civil society–international institution partnership that offered a concrete example of how the global community could work together to resolve common problems. Other similar efforts emerged that resulted in the creation of the International Criminal Court and the movement to curb the use of children as soldiers.

From these efforts has emerged the nucleus of a movement that seeks to enhance global security not by increasing the number of weapons being developed, produced, and traded in an already over-weaponized world, but by addressing "human security" needs as the fundamental linchpin upon which rests all security. Human security concepts hold that by addressing the basic needs of the majority on the planet, and providing the majority with a stake in and hope for their own future, the root causes of conflict are diminished. Dialogue, cross-cultural understanding, and conflict resolution enhance human security. Globalized relations, interaction, and communication enhance human security. The resort to force is not scorned, but it is recognized as the absolute last resort and a clear recognition of a failure of all other methods to resolve conflict.

The New Global Enemy

Even as this new thinking was developing, pressure to continue to think and act in old ways was building. Old systems of nation-to-nation interaction die hard, and some nations sought to diminish or eliminate completely the role of new actors in addressing global issues. The human security agenda was painted as wishy-washy efforts by "lesser powers" – read irrelevant – who did not have the military might or the "spine" to deal with real security issues. These global realists also argued that national security issues are too complex for mere civilians to understand, let alone have a voice in.

In this context, the Al Qaeda network began to emerge as a recognized threat with the first attack on the World Trade Towers in New York in 1993. US forces in Saudi Arabia were attacked at Khobar Towers in 1996. The US embassies in Kenya and Tanzania were bombed in 1998. In 2000, the *USS Cole* was attacked while docked in Yemen for refueling. All these are examples of asymmetrical tools of terror employed to advance the political goals of a changed Middle East free of Western dominance, terror most horrifically displayed in the September 11 attacks in New York and Washington.

Sometimes, as when Mr Bush declared his new "crusade" in the volatile and emotional days immediately following those terrorist attacks, it is made very clear that it is "us against them," and it is very clear who "they" are. Other times, with public protestations that the new enemy is not any and all people of Arabic origin or who are members of the Islamic faith, the contours of the new "evil" are less clear. Yet, as Israel builds its wall to cordon off some of occupied Palestine in response to the second intifada, that wall for many in the world represents a new physical expression of a barrier against the new global enemy: an Islamic terror network. Some of the enemy are seen as clear opponents holding or desiring to hold and defend territory. Others are considered even more dangerous, a "shadowy" network spreading its tentacles through cells and organizations in an increasing number of countries in the world. No matter how it is portrayed, it is always insinuated that we are faced with an enemy as vast and as threatening as the Communist bloc used to be, which will require all the will and resources of the "free world" to vanquish as well.

Is Endless War the Best Answer?

As we know all too well, the tremendous support around the world for the people of the United States in response to the terrorist attacks of September 11 has largely been squandered through the essentially unilateral invasion of Iraq, based on twisted truths, false assumptions, and little meaningful preparation for the post-Hussein occupation of that country. While people were united in their sorrow and disgust at the terrorism of September 11, many hoped the global unity in the aftermath of the attacks would result in a different type of leadership to respond to the attacks. Many wanted governments to work together not only to dismantle the terrorist network and bring the perpetrators of such attacks to justice, but also to diffuse tensions by beginning to seriously address the root causes of the problems that made recruiting for such networks possible. But the clash of ideologies seeking dominance in and over the Middle East has shattered that hope and placed us all at greater risk.

Certainly there is a clash of some sort going on. Terrorism is a threat that must be countered, whether it be terrorism practiced by an individual, a group, or a state. But is terrorism, and the response to it, truly a manifestation of a clash of civilizations? How much is the clash attributable to manipulation of culture and religion for political/ideological ends, whatever the religious or ideological stripe of the manipulator? How much is fueled and stoked in order to provide a continued justification for huge military expenditures and taxpayer subsidies for the arms industry, as well as justification for "reluctant" global dominance. War and preparations for war are presented as the only answer to the new global threat.

In such a worldview, what room is there for new approaches to the ongoing problems at the root of the clash? Indeed, even debate and discussion of current policies in the "greatest of the world's democracies" often seems barely tolerated. Questioning the "war on terror" or what might propel people to strap bombs on themselves in gross acts of terrorism against innocent civilians is suspect, smacking perhaps even of treason. Calls for dialogue, for negotiated resolution of conflicts, or for meaningful multilateral approaches to address our common human security are dismissed as wildly utopian and barely worthy of consideration.

But dismissing calls for reasoned discussion, analysis, and multilateralism as utopian is, in my view, a means to quash all debate and an attempt to control outcomes. Despite the gross failures of intelligence and leadership pre-9/11, again in the lead-up to the invasion of Iraq and the obvious failure of planning for that country in a post-Hussein environment, we are still expected to suspend our disbelief and accept that it is a "wise few" with access to information to which the rest of us are not privy who really can resolve the threats to our common security.

I believe that if we want to avert the transformation of dealing with terrorism into a "clash of civilizations," we must change the way we think, the way we talk, and the way we approach the problems of the world – including the global threat of terrorism. Understanding the terrorist threat does not mean simply being able to identify the countries from which the terrorists come. We must understand the underlying, competing political forces that result in people being willing to die and take innocents with them to make a political and ideological point. In a world increasingly dominated by the few, who give the perception of not caring much for the many, asymmetrical responses will likely seem the only way to equalize the playing field. Until we work together as a global community to address the common threats to human security posed by these gross inequalities, we will not live in a secure world.

But if we are indeed a global community, the world cannot wait for one power, no matter what that power might be, to determine our common future. Just as they did in the landmine ban movement or in the creation of the International Criminal Court, like-minded governments must expand their leadership and make common cause with international institutions and with civil society to seek new ways to address challenges to our common security. No one government, no one entity, can possibly provide for the needs of us all.

A call for new coalitions to seek new solutions is not an attempt to isolate, but it is a call to not abdicate individual and collective responsibility for our future. The call to challenge accepted thinking about how to address violence or the myriad challenges to human security is in some ways an echo of the words of 52 British diplomats who wrote a public letter to their Prime Minister in April 2004 expressing their alarm at the policies of their government toward Iraq and Israel. In calling for a policy review, they wrote: "We share your view that the British government has an interest in working as closely as possible with the United States on both these related issues, and in exerting real influence as a loyal ally. We believe that the need for such influence is now a matter of the highest urgency. If that is unacceptable or unwelcome there is no case for supporting policies which are doomed to failure."

Those who do not accept collective punishment as a just response to violence or continued pursuit of flawed policies simply because they are in place must accept the challenge of working to create space for different solutions. Change will not happen overnight. But that must not be an excuse for inaction. It is possible to reverse the slide to further ideologically driven division and increased violence. Almost anything is possible when there is sufficient will. Some would contend that in these difficult and uncertain times, building such will is impossible. Often, it takes only a handful of people to be catalyst to real and meaningful change. As the poet Theodore Roethke said, "What we need is more people who specialize in the impossible."

10

Dialogue among Civilizations and Cultures

President Seyed Mohammed Khatami

Effective engagement in a dialogue among civilizations and across cultures requires an understanding of essential concepts and relationships. One of the most basic of these is the relationship between dialogue and knowledge. Knowledge is the product of dialogue and exchange: *speaking* and *listening*. Once complemented by *seeing*, they constitute the most important physical, mental, and spiritual faculties and activities of human beings. Seeing expands the realm of knowing; it strengthens and solidifies the self. One talks to others and listens to others, but seeing is realized from the vantage point of the *self* and the world, and humans become the subject matter of the self. Speaking and listening, on the other hand, are efforts by two or more parties aimed at coming closer to truth and achieving understanding. That is why dialogue is neither the metier of skeptics nor the property of those claiming monopoly over truth. Rather, it reveals its beautiful but veiled face only to those aspirants who march hand in hand and shoulder to shoulder with other human beings.

The concept of dialogue among civilizations and cultures is based on such a definition of truth, and is not in conflict with philosophical definitions of truth. Nor is it principally about speaking. In effective dialogue among civilizations, listening is as important as speaking.

Speaking and listening require addressing. It is only through addressing that words are spoken and heard. The question begs itself: When and in what status is man addressed? In other words, what is the realm where addressing takes place? Not in the realm of science; science represents a conscious, deliberate effort toward discovering the relations and arrangements among things. Scientific statements do not venture beyond or beneath human consciousness. The realm of art and religion, in contrast, are the realms of addressing and intention. Works of art address us, as does religion. Divine words address human beings. That is why mystical and religious languages are so deeply and fundamentally interconnected, and no wonder that early artistic works by human beings are also considered "sacred art." The call "O People" recurs often in the Bible and in the Qur'an; the concept of the People is discussed at a personified level. The word "person" shares etymologically the same Latin origin as the "mask" or "persona" of actors in dramatic plays. In religious addressing, when man is the addressee of the divine word, and not in particular situations where specific religious injunctions are made, it is the true, metahistorical and unitary essence of man that is being addressed. Hence, divine religions are not in conflict in their fundamental essence and message; their differences relate only to legal injunctions and the particular laws and regulations pertaining to social and legal specifics.

There is, of course, a distinct danger of exaggerated optimism for immediate results emanating from the proposal for dialogue among civilizations and cultures. This could be as disappointing as exaggerated pessimism, overemphasis on the dismal actual state of affairs in the world and impediments in the way of such dialogue. Therefore, we should all be cognizant of, and fully prepared for, the long meandering and highly treacherous trajectory that lies ahead of us in pursuit of dialogue. Keeping these difficulties and barriers in view, we should constantly explore the possibility of a humane course for history and the future of mankind as this new paradigm develops. The fact that this proposal was welcomed by the international community, and specifically lauded at the United Nations General Assembly by the collective of its member states, as well as by intellectuals and world public opinion, is in itself important and valuable. World public opinion, as we know, does not always or easily subscribe in earnest to calls for change.

"Dialogue among civilizations and cultures" can be explained and interpreted in different ways at different levels. Nevertheless, reflection on the very meaning of dialogue – interlocution – is essential for paving the way for an appropriate discussion, which requires entering into philosophical and historical discussions and considering the views of great thinkers on this concept. One aspect of this cannot be overlooked: that dialogue has two meanings, real and virtual. When we call on the world for dialogue, it could inevitably involve both meanings.

The idea of dialogue among civilizations and cultures may seem to have brought together a compendium of apparently conflicting or even contradictory characteristics. On the one hand, it is as old as the human civilization and culture itself. On the other hand, it is a rather new and novel idea. It should not be difficult to resolve the apparent conflict. A literalist could define "dialogue among civilizations" in a way that signifies its old age, while the traditionalist could define "culture," "civilization," and "man" in a manner concordant with an emphasis on the collective aspect of human existence and an emphasis on the general, unbounded, and expansive nature of culture and civilization, consistent with the idea that no culture or civilization has emerged in isolation from others. The aspects of cultures that have survived are those that have had the capacity for exchange, and especially for listening. Listening is a virtue to be acquired; its acquisition needs purposeful moral training, self-refining, and rational nurturing. Listening is not a passive act like silence; it is, rather, an activity through which listeners expose themselves to the world of others, the interlocutors. Without listening, any dialogue is doomed to failure.

Understanding "dialogue among civilizations" descriptively carries a number of implications, one of which impinges on the relationship between statesman and artist and another on that between ethics and politics. What, indeed, is the relationship between a great statesman and a consummate artist? How, in particular, are they similar and congruent? Politicking is a form of art, but the artist is one who can live in the present and make it permanent. It takes a great artist to be able to create a type of permanence in a work of art so that we can understand that work in its proper time and place. The historical destiny of great art is thus established through permanence. Similarly, the historical destiny of different nations and societies is often shaped in the hands of epoch-making great statesmen.

Creativity is another quality shared by statesman and artist alike. It implies novelty, where repetition and imitation have no place. The full realization of the creative quality in man depends on courage, a moral attribute. Great artists take on artistic truth with creativity and valor, and great statesmen take on their country's critical affairs with the same qualities. In their efforts to create dialogue among civilizations, statesmen today should take a fundamental step forward for a more just and humane future.

And what is the relevance of ethics and politics to the dialogue among cultures? The theoretical aspect of this relationship has received much attention. Of particular relevance and significance here is the ethical aspect of the proposal. To realize dialogue among cultures, a fundamental change in political ethics is essential and inevitable. Participation, fulfillment of obligation, and humility are primary ethical attributes needed for the realization of the dialogue among civilizations in politics and international relations. Governments that rely on economic, material, and military might to arrogate to themselves the logic of force, imposition, and deceit in pursuit of their interests should yield to the logic of dialogue. What is needed is not change in language and terminology alone, but substantive change in relationships and arrangements as well. Rational thinking should merge and mingle with human emotion. The essence of Sa'adi's poem should be taken to heart, that "human beings are parts of the same body, for they are of the same essence in creation." This is as much needed in national life as in the international arena. Should such a welcome change come about through the efforts of well-meaning philanthropic thinkers and artists, we will not be dealing any more with the plastic language dominating international diplomacy. We will be dealing instead with a lively and dynamic and, more importantly, ethical and humane language.

"Dialogue" is used here in its precise meaning, different from such terms of general meaning as "cultural and civilizational exchange" or impact. The two should not be confused. Mutual impact in the realm of culture and civilization, as well as cultural and scientific exchange, could be based on war and conquest. History tells us that the imposition of a single culture or civilization on the competitors and contenders has been achieved at times through resort to brute force, and in our days mostly through communications technology. Therefore, dialogue as we understand it and as discussed here can be realized and achieved once premised on particular philosophical, ethical, and psychological dispositions. So defense of dialogue cannot be based on any *Weltanschauung* (world outlook) or belief in a philosophical, religious, political, or ethical system. For dialogue to take place we need a set of a priori and comprehensive general axioms, without which dialogue in the precise sense of the word would be impossible. Research in, and articulation of, such axioms and their propagation on a global scale could, and should, be undertaken by such venerable institutions as UNESCO. Such axioms and the essence of the proposal of "dialogue among civilizations" are as much in conflict with the dogmatic axioms of positivists and the absolutes of modernists as they are with the unlimited skepticisms of the post-moderns. It is therefore incumbent on thinkers supporting the idea of dialogue among civilizations and cultures to refine its philosophical and theoretical foundations, to safeguard it against the onslaught of dogmatic enmity to any possibility of reaching truth, and prevent it from submersion in the limitless skepticism of the post-modern thinkers – who, far removed from the unfathomable pain and suffering of millions of deprived and wretched people, judge any struggle for justice and against oppression to be a particular genre of meta-discursive philosophical explanation.

Tolerance is another important prerequisite for the dialogue among civilizations. Tolerance is essential for the very initial stages of dialogue, yet there is a huge difference between negative tolerance as espoused in the post-modern era and the positive harmony cherished by religions and philosophies of the East. For dialogue to become a new paradigm for our world, the foundation must be elevated from negative tolerance to positive, shared concord. The Holy Qur'an enjoins Muslims to "cooperate in beneficence and virtue" (chapter V, 2). All members of the human community have the right, and should be able in reality, to cooperate and collaborate with each other in constructing the world in which they are living at the beginning of this third millennium. No people or nation should be excluded or marginalized in this day and age by means of resort to any philosophical, political, or economic justification. Others should not just be tolerated; rather, they should be interacted with. The global community should be the product of the cooperation of the entire human community. This might have sounded a romantic slogan at the turn of the twentieth century or even a few years back; it is now an inescapable necessity for the survival of mankind.

This concept of cooperation and collaboration is not only of a social, political, or economic nature. To bring the hearts of people closer together, we need first to bring their minds together. Belief in conflicting philosophical, ethical, or religious principles militates against the hopes for such closeness of hearts. Fellowship and closeness among hearts thus needs fellowship and closeness among minds, and this can be achieved only through the painstaking efforts of great thinkers understanding the fundamentals of the minds of others and their subsequent elaboration and explication among their own people. We all need to engage in a serious exchange on the fundamental meanings and concepts of thinking and feeling. All of us need to explain and elucidate our own meanings of such concepts as "salvation," "life," and "death." Such a venture may eschew producing immediate or even short-term results, yet in its absence any agreement based solely on economic or political interests would prove fragile and transient.

The twentieth century, much to our collective chagrin, was perhaps the worst period in all human history in terms of war, bloodshed, oppression, and exploitation. Its positive aspects and achievements were the collective outcome of the thinking of great thinkers and policies of great statesmen. Overcoming the agony and horrors of the past century can be achieved only through substantive change in the fundamentals of political thinking and through effective replacement of the prevailing paradigm in international relations with that of the dialogue among civilizations and cultures.

11

Transnational Moral Dialogues

Amitai Etzioni

Beyond a general trend to develop a global normative synthesis of a set of core values, a process has developed that enables people of different nations, from both the East and the West, to come to shared moral understandings on specific issues. These issues range from values that drive the movement to ban landmines, to the quest to curb the warming of the Earth, to the condemnation of child pornography, to opposition to the invasion of sovereign countries. These shared understandings, in turn, serve to feed a worldwide public opinion. This does not mean that everyone is informed or involved, let alone in agreement with one another. Even in developed and democratic nations, what is called the attentive public – those who follow public affairs and form judgments about public policies – does not amount to more than a fraction of the population, and consensus is never complete. Still, the overwhelming majority of the attentive public can lean in one direction or another and have an effect on the course of public affairs. What follow are a few lines about the processes involved, which I refer to as moral dialogues.

Moral dialogues occur when a group of people engage in a process of sorting out the values that should guide their lives. The values involved are not necessarily such personal values as veracity, modesty, and honesty, but ones that affect what public policies people favor, either in their own country or in others. These matters include affirmative action, the treatment of asylum seekers, the recognition of gay marriages, whether the death penalty should be imposed, and much more.

Moral dialogues are often messy; they meander and have no clean beginnings or endings. They are passionate and often contentious. Nevertheless, over time they often lead to new shared understandings, which in turn deeply affect not merely what people believe but also their actions, not only what people consider virtuous but also the habits of their hearts. Among the most telling examples are the development of a moral commitment to the environment following moral dialogues initiated by the publication of Rachel Carson's book *Silent Spring*; the change in the ways people viewed relations between men and women following moral dialogues initiated by the publication of Betty Friedan's *The Feminist Mystique*; the changes in race relations that followed moral dialogues initiated by the civil rights movement in the 1960s; and the nearly self-enforcing ban on smoking in public in the United States after prolonged moral dialogues about the ill effects of smoking on nonsmokers.

It is easy to demonstrate that such dialogues take place constantly – and often productively – in well-formed national societies, which most democracies are, and that frequently they result, albeit sometimes only after prolonged dialogues, in a new normative direction for these societies. But can such moral dialogues take place transnationally, and if so, to what effect? It is these dialogues that are most relevant to both the general development of the global normative synthesis and to the formulation of specific shared moral understandings that can undergird specific public policies. Granted, transnational moral dialogues are much more limited than their intranational counterparts in scope, intensity, conclusion, and result. Nevertheless, they are beginning to provide a wider shared moral understanding, political culture, and legitimacy for transnational institutions than existed until recently. For example, transnational dialogues that have concluded that "we" ought to respect women's rights, promote democracy, and prevent superpowers from acting without "our" consent.

True, such dialogues are affected by numerous nonnormative considerations, often dressed up as normative claims. Nevertheless, these dialogues do affect what people of different nationalities consider to be morally appropriate. Thus, one reason most countries try to avoid being perceived as environmentally irresponsible is that they do not wish to be seen as acting illegitimately in the eyes of other nations.[1] Moreover, transnational moral dialogues occur on three levels. Should the people of one culture "judge" those of others? If yes, which values should guide such judgments? And what means should be employed, beyond speech and symbolic gestures, to undergird these values? For instance, there is much stronger agreement that terror should be curbed than there is about which means are best used to do so.

Of all the global dialogues, particularly significant for the issues at hand are those that concern the developing new global architectures. Currently, the most important dialogue along these lines focuses on the key question: Under which conditions is it legitimate – that is, in line with shared values, mores, and laws – for one nation, or a group of nations, to employ force in order to interfere in the internal affairs of other nations? Few observers still accept the principle that what happens in a nation is of no matter to others, that nation-states are sovereign in their own turf, that the principle of *self*-determination should be upheld; and that no other nation has a right to apply force to intervene. The growing recognition of basic human rights has led many to believe that other nations, the United Nations, and in a sense the world community have not merely a right but also a duty to encourage, if need be to pressure, and if all else fails to use force to protect these rights.[2]

There is growing worldwide moral support for intervention for humanitarian purposes. Various powerful nations, and some that are not particularly powerful, have been roundly chided for not having intervened to stop the genocide in Rwanda, in which some 800,000 people were killed and many others maimed. This has been true also of genocide in the Congo and elsewhere.[3] There is a growing normative brief for a court that would try individuals who commit the most serious violations of international humanitarian law, such as genocide – specifically, for the International Criminal Court.

In addition, there is a surprisingly strong shared opposition to unilateral action. Many in both the East and the West prefer action by groups of nations, coalitions in which all the members are consulted and each has a veto power, as occurs in NATO. Further, many support action that has been endorsed by the United Nations and is in line with international law. The motivation that leads many heads of state and citizens alike to favor such positions often may have little to do with moral considerations. Rather, the motivation may reflect the desire of weak powers to curb the more powerful ones, especially the superpower, or the desire of nations that were once major players on the world stage, such as France and Russia, to regain influence on the global scene or to win an election at home (as Chancellor Gerhard Schroeder did in Germany, and as Roh Moo Hyun did in South Korea in 2003). Nevertheless, the fact that those opposed to unilateral activity can find huge audiences that are receptive to their claims that the United Nations should be respected (despite its numerous and serious limitations), that multilateralism is preferable to unilateralism, and that compliance with international laws is important (despite their vagueness and fungibility) shows the direction in which shared moral understandings are evolving. The same leaders might well have made the opposite claims if those would have served their political goals. The ways in which they are fashioning their arguments reveal the directions in which shared transnational values are evolving as a result of global moral dialogues.

To argue that there are evolving transnational shared moral understandings, which in turn affect what the public is willing to accept as legitimate acts and institutions, is not to suggest that global public opinion is all-powerful or even that it is highly effective. Military force still plays a key role and can be applied in defiance of worldviews. Economic factors also play a key role, as evidenced when national governments change direction after they are promised large amounts of loans, grants, or foreign aid, concessions in tariffs, and so on. Still, public opinion is one significant factor that affects how much normative power a nation commands and which acts and institutions are considered legitimate. Flying in the face of this opinion has both short- and long-term costs. Moreover, if the developments of global institutions follow their current course, the effect of world public opinion on the future direction of global public affairs will grow in importance. Followers of what might be called the Madison Avenue school believe that public opinion can be manipulated through a series of clever ads, Voice of America broadcasts, and colorful brochures.[4] Advocates of this view, for instance, "believe that blitzing Arab and Muslim countries with Britney Spears videos and Arabic-language sitcoms will earn Washington millions of new Muslim sympathizers."[5] Ads can be used to change people's attitudes from favoring one brand of consumer goods to another, say Pepsi over Coke, especially when the difference between them is minimal, and many millions of dollars are spent on such campaigns. But when it comes to moral issues, many factors drive public opinion, including religious upbringing, education, communal pressures, and independent media sources. True, public opinion can sometimes be misled and misdirected. However, a superpower, or for that matter any power that proceeds on the assumption that it can shape public opinion by Madison Avenue devices, often will find, to its chagrin, that people's views have an independent force of their own. Hence the importance of the evolving global synthesis, not merely for general normative purposes but also as a key element in developing what is considered a legitimate new global architecture.[6]

Notes

1 Gareth Porter and Janet Welsh Brown, *Global Environmental Politics* (Boulder, CO: Westview Press, 1996), pp. 69–105; Beth Simmons, "International Law and State Behavior: Commitment and Compliance in International Monetary Affairs," *American Political Science Review*, 94/4 (2000): 819–35.

2 Charles Taylor argues that there is a voluntary global consensus on human rights, though different cultures may disagree on the justifications for these universal norms. See Charles Taylor, "Conditions of an Unforced Consensus on Human Rights," in *The East Asian Challenge for Human Rights*, ed. Joanne R. Bauer and Daniel A. Bell (New York: Cambridge University Press, 1999).

3 Barbara Harff, "No Lessons Learned from the Holocaust? Assessing Risks of Genocide and Political Mass Murder Since 1955," *American Political Science Review*, 97/1 (2003): 57–73.

4 Several groups have begun to push for a "public diplomacy" solution to the perceived growth in anti-Americanism around the world. For instance, Christopher Ross writes, "I am delighted with the burgeoning recognition that how the U.S. government communicates abroad – and with whom – directly affects the nation's security and well-being." See Christopher Ross, "Public Diplomacy Comes of Age," *Washington Quarterly*, 25/2 (Spring 2002): 75; Antony J. Blinken, "Winning the War of Ideas," *Washington Quarterly*, 25/2 (Spring 2002): 101–14; and *Finding America's Voice: A Strategy for Reinvigorating U.S. Public Diplomacy*, The Council on Foreign Relations Independent Task Force Report (New York: The Council on Foreign Relations, 2003).

5 Robert Satloff, "How to Win Friends and Influence Arabs," *Weekly Standard*, August 18, 2003, p. 18.

6 Amitai Etzioni, *From Empire to Community* (New York: Palgrave, 2004).

12

In Other People's Shoes

Dame Marilyn Strathern

People seem to find it very easy to make divisions among themselves. No end of examples spring to mind, whether one thinks of divisions between nations or villages, religions or neighbors. The social anthropologist's notebooks are full of instances. But then so is anyone's. Divisions can alienate and create problems, but the problems lie not in division itself. The capacity of people to divide themselves off from one another is a highly creative and productive resource. In fact, it is the foundation of the capacity to make relationships. So where have we gone wrong?

Let me spell out the inspiration for the question. It comes not from observing events on the world stage but from the countless studies social anthropologists have undertaken with people whose world stage does not get into the headlines and whose capacity for hostility and injury is often very restricted in scale. That does not make their ferocity any less savage than that of countries with long-distance arsenals at their disposal, but it does bring to light aspects of division one might otherwise overlook. Of course scale is tricky: there are many more small-scale acts of savagery in the so-called civilized world than there are large-scale ones, as the victims of sexual violence will tell you. And to someone who falls ill from sorcery or whose children are hacked with machetes, life comes crashing down every bit as painfully as it did for the Germans burnt by Allied bombers from thousands of feet in the air.

We shall not do ourselves any good by imagining that anywhere people live without conflict. There are better and worse ways of dealing with it, and more and less subtle ways of avoiding escalation before it becomes damaging. But conflict is built on one of the essential ingredients of relating – division – and it is imperative that we recognize this. For we need to find ways of seeing division for what it is.

By division I mean the capacity for people to differentiate themselves from one another. Division implies a previous relationship, even if only by proximity. It underlies the way we translate humanity into social life. Social life consists largely in making distinctions as much as it consists in drawing analogies. Anthropologists interested in the evolution of family and kinship would say that at its core lies the differentiation of persons from one another, and thus the perception that between persons lies something that may be variously imagined as a bond or tie. Putting oneself in someone else's shoes is a powerful analogy. But the shoes remain definitely someone else's. The perspective that the other person has on me is reciprocal to the perspective I have on her, but it is not identical. If we were identical, there could be no exchange of perspectives.

In fact, being taken as identical may be regarded as something to be carefully avoided. We find this, for instance, in protocols surrounding succession. An heir should not succeed before his time. A well-known rule in parts of West Africa is that the eldest son should never look into his father's granary. The son must be held at arm's length from, and thus divided from, the father, something first learnt when he was little, and be forbidden to eat from the same spoon. To do so would be to anticipate the father's absence and thus death, for the concomitant assumption is that it is the son who will after his death literally step into his shoes. This initial division helps to manage the reproductive or generative traffic between the generations.

Social life comes from the capacity to see that relations are analogous to other relations, that my tie with my mother is like her tie with her mother. It is in this second-order extrapolation that anthropologists recognize human sociality. It becomes possible to think about relations between relations, and to imagine the consequences of complex interrelations. It also becomes possible to think about relationships in the abstract. Here we see certain powers and abilities ascribed to people in different roles. Otherwise it might seem bizarre that anyone should think it necessary to turn boys and girls into men and women, as happens through initiation rituals across the world. But it can become very necessary in anticipation of their future joining together as husband and wife, when the difference between the sexes becomes an analogy for the distinct contributions that different sets of kin make to future generations. The future is held to lie in bringing together what first must be divided, made separate.

But why so much effort to separate? The effort is most evident in activities that take sameness as their premise. People are fundamentally the same, and it is a moral responsibility to differentiate them. Sameness in the background leads to an exaggeration of difference that becomes the basis of relationships. The alternative premise is that difference is what one takes for granted. People are different in nature, and it is a moral responsibility to create fundamental similarities.

The paradox is that those who take the premise of similarity are quite as capable of uniting, but they tend to do so on other grounds. The grounds are basically those of the division of labor: people come to depend on one another when they have different tasks to do, and cooperate or make a unified project out of the differences themselves. So it is not the capacity to cooperate or unite that is in question. Rather, there are alternative ways of justifying or representing joint activity: the exaggeration of difference and suppression of identity in order to make the need for interdependence obvious (division of labor model), or the exaggeration of similarity and suppression of difference in order to bind through a common goal (aim for unity model).

This applies as well in larger social domains. We live in a world in which nation-states and sectarian institutions generally feel they must aim for cooperation and consensus in the face of difference. The paradox remains: Difference is always in the background. Too much rhetoric of sameness breeds fear of difference, regurgitates terrible images of heathens and infidels and the need for "homeland security," brands aliens as "evil" and "other," sees only threat in strangers. What might be benign when people appeal to a spirit of community becomes lethal when the borders are patrolled and rampant familism keeps the unwanted out.

Because the approach to unity via sameness has center stage in global media, I stress the alternative route to unity: that is, via value put on difference. Think for a moment about dialogue. Dialogue is not just a matter of diversity and of encompassing different points of view. It is also about argument. The media is a morass of points of view, with opinions relayed from every vantage point imaginable. But while you can adopt a viewpoint and relay it, you cannot argue from one. There is no competition. In order to argue, you need to have detached yourself from – divided yourself off from – competing positions you might have occupied; that is, from yourself standing in another person's shoes. We might say that such management of perspectives is the essence of argument. Paradoxically, the more engaged the argument, the more ground the protagonists make between them. If world civilizations feel besieged, and if lack of mutual knowledge fuels this, we need more than ever to nourish our practices of debate and critique, to make our wisdom Socratic. Not pluralistic but dialogic. A dream, but how wonderful if people going hammer and tongs for one another in argument came to the conclusion that their differences were only academic!

Nothing can do away with the social fact that everyone has different interests, and is propelled by different visions. We forget that it is often the differences that compel us to act. When social action requires the active shedding of alternatives and the dividing of one's interests from others in order to deal with both, the entity being divided is the relation between the parties. Argument is an important form of relating in this sense.

It is because this kind of difference is so much more than diversity that I have used the term "division." Division does not always have a pretty outcome. Enemies are "divided" when they define their targets in relation to one another. In the asymmetrical division of developed and developing world, the price for interdependence may be the highly exploitable dependency of some on others. Yet division is not itself a value or moral precept – it is a ubiquitous social practice. But it also makes something workable, something of a tool, out of difference.

One cannot, should not, eliminate difference. One can work with it. Men from the highlands of Papua New Guinea coming as unemployed migrants to Port Moresby taught me that. Here was the immigrant, in a city full of strangers, where it was impossible to tell friend from foe, everyone had a fierce loyalty to their home group, and there were few common rules. He would do everything he could to differentiate himself from them. Yet on the premise of similarity the new urban resident assumed that in the same way as he himself had interests, loyalties, obligations, so too did the strangers he knew nothing about. However helpful or treacherous they turned out to be, he did them the credit of assuming that, like him, they were caught up in a social world with its own moralities. This is putting oneself in someone else's shoes; this is analogic thinking. It is the courtesy that allows one to engage with a world full of people with whom one has practically nothing in common, but almost everything in parallel. A route to dialogue.

13

A Universal Language, without Boundary or Prejudice

Sir Ravi Shankar

Learning that so many eminent people were going to contribute their essays on the subject of clash of humanity, I was at a loss where and how to start and surprised that I was even asked. As a musician, my main language for expression is music. That is what I'll try to do, write this essay about my musical language.

Thousands of years ago when man started to invent fire to cook, tools to hunt, clothes to protect, seeds for crops, and plow for food, he also learned to appreciate and imitate birds, and through his voice taught himself to sing, thump his feet to dance for happy occasions and rituals. He drew on the cave walls all that he saw around him. Gradually the crude original forms of drums, wind, bowed, and plucked instruments came into existence. It is amazing how it was only the human who had this inventiveness and creativity and no other living being.

From the time mankind started to be in awe and worshiped the sun, the fire, and other great forces of nature, he gradually invented and learned a lot of things like building houses and roads, irrigation and agriculture, how to make and use varieties of clothes and ornaments, as well as develop spoken and written languages. But most important of all, by then he invented God! There developed different religious beliefs in different parts of the world: initially pagan and ritualistic, then gradually more sophisticated, philosophical, and spiritual. We know of the height of cultural development in the lands of China, India, Egypt, Greece, Rome, and elsewhere.

With these developments came the discovery of the need for adjustment. On my sitar each string needs fine-tuning. If each string is fine-tuned, then the chords and harmony fall into place, eliminating discord and disharmony which create cacophony. One needs to be in tune with oneself before trying to fine-tune anybody else.

An able leader can do the great task with his tremendous ideas and ability to execute them with the love he gives and receives from the people. We had a few such ideal leaders throughout our history, but unfortunately most of them turned out to be dictators. Lust for power and wealth made them ruthless and ruined all that they built.

It is very obvious that with all the technological developments, the average person is getting the advantage of material comforts along with information and entertainment through the internet and television more than ever. Great social thinkers everywhere seem to be wondering where the effect of these sudden social changes are going to lead us, especially our younger generation.

Each generation witnesses such change. I saw it happen in the United States and the United Kingdom, mostly from the early 1960s. The Beatniks were already there. They were mostly over 35. As writers, painters, musicians, actors, and other entertainers, most of them were achievers and well known. They also experienced drugs. Then came the period of poetry readings, ballad singing, and folk clubs. That's when it all started, the young boys and girls joined in caravan, growing long beards and hair, using fancy and exotic dresses and beads, and using patchouli scent to cover the strong smell of grass and hash. Many of them were also on higher trips on LSD, mushrooms, and other strong chemicals. My agents in the UK and the USA had booked me to play in folk clubs in 1966 and 1967. That is where I first experienced these characters who seemed to be from another planet. Though they appreciated and loved me so much, I didn't feel happy, and felt myself and my music being soiled. This is because I received my music from my guru (Baba Allaudin), who followed a musical tradition which associated itself with spirituality and against drugs and alcohol.

Though I was already well known from 1956 onward, performing in large and prestigious halls all over Europe and America, George Harrison becoming my student in 1966 added to my sudden big popularity with the young people. The kids started loving and admiring me as a pop star. Playing in large arenas and open air concerts I was unhappy with almost all of the stoned hippy audiences. They were raucous and high-charged youngsters behaving as they would do in a pop or rock concert. The essence of incense sticks that I always burn on stage in my recitals to create the instant atmosphere of temples and spiritual India was submerged by the strong smell of hash and patchouli.

For those few years between 1967 and 1973 I constantly told my young listeners in my concerts, TV, radio, and journals that I was against young people using drugs, particularly associating them with music, yoga, meditation, or any serious pursuit in life. I used to tell them that one didn't drink alcohol and get drunk to go to a concert or church. One can do whatever one wants for fun and frolic, but have restraint and respect for the higher and serious values in life, and don't associate drugs with them. The listeners who are still there are the most appreciative and discerning listeners of Indian music all over the world today. Gone are those days of ignorance in the West when they clapped after a couple of minutes of fine-tuning of our instruments or appreciated tuning the right-hand drum of the Tabla by striking it with the hammer, thinking it was part of the music piece.

I came here as an Indian musician to share the great music of my country with the rest of the world. It was a difficult path in the beginning, but with my zeal and dedication to preserving the spirituality in my music I feel that my music has been able to touch so many. Indian music has such great force both intellectually, as well as aesthetically or spiritually. I feel happy and honored that great musicians such as Yehudi Menuhin, Mstislav Rostropovich, Jean-Pierre Rampal, John Coltrane, George Harrison, Philip Glass, Buddy Rich, Paul Horn, Bud Shank and Hosan Yamamoto, and Musumi Miyashita played compositions (either with me or without) learned from me, or were greatly influenced by me. I enjoyed my association with André Previn for my Sitar Concerto No. 1 with Orchestra (1970) and Zubin Mehta for the Sitar Concerto No. 2 (1980).

Experiments around the world have shown and proven that using music, including mine, make plants grow better, blood pressures lower, and even animals behave better. It is my wish that music is introduced in all schools in every corner of the world. It is every child's basic right to have the opportunity to learn music, as it enhances their development in a more positive way than education without music. We are trying to work towards this through my center in Delhi in whatever small way we can.

It is my strong belief that if only all the political leaders of the world and officers of power in all sectors were a little musical, there would have been less violence and bloodshed and more harmony on this planet. Music is a universal language with no boundaries or prejudices. I have tried to use this language to speak to people all over the world, hoping to touch their hearts, minds, and imaginations with the spirituality that is within Indian classical music when performed by a true, dedicated artist. It has the power to heal, uplift the human spirit, and bring peace. I am grateful that I have had the opportunity to contribute toward these goals. If my music has had any positive influence, helped anyone find a small measure of contentment, or inspired others to express love or know peace, then I know that my vision for a better world is coming into focus, and that music is an integral and beautiful dialogue in this essential venture.

14

Dialogue among Civilizations

Kofi Annan

The United Nations was created in the belief that dialogue can triumph over discord, that diversity is a universal virtue, and that the peoples of the world are far more united by their common fate than they are divided by their separate identities. This is a tall order; after all civilizations and cultures are not constant or immutable facts of history. Rather, they are organisms in constant flux: always changing, growing, and adapting themselves to new times and new realities through interaction with each other. Nor do they necessarily coincide with a particular religious belief. It is a gross oversimplification to speak of a Christian or Muslim or Buddhist civilization; doing so only creates boundaries where none need exist.

Indeed, generalizations about civilizations cannot stand the test of modern times. Migration, integration, and technology are bringing different races, cultures, and ethnicities closer together, breaking down old barriers and creating new realities. We are, as never before, the products of many influences. We live, as never before, with both the foreign and the familiar.

This is not to suggest that we cannot rightly take pride in our particular heritage or faith. We can, and we should. But the notion that what is "ours" is necessarily in conflict with what is "theirs" is both false and dangerous. We can love what we are without hating what we are not.

In what sense, then, is the dialogue among civilizations a useful concept? First, it is an appropriate and necessary answer to the notion of an inevitable clash of civilizations. As such, it provides a vehicle for advancing cooperation. Second, and most important, the dialogue can help us distinguish lies from facts, and propaganda from sound analysis. This can be especially helpful in uncovering the real grievances that lie at the heart of conflict.

The Balkans over the past decade have provided us with grim and tragic examples of the uses and misuses of history to further division and conflict. There, what could be termed a dialogue among civilizations which had taken place for centuries was violently destroyed. Suddenly, the Muslims of Bosnia were referred to as "Turks," and their persecution justified by what their alleged ancestors had allegedly done 500 years ago. In this case, a clearer understanding of history, of culture, and of religion could have helped the transition from communism to democracy, and genuine issues of rights and responsibilities could have been addressed in a pluralist environment based on mutual respect.

In the Middle East, already delicate issues of territory, nationhood, and ownership have been rendered even more complex by religious differences, centered on a land holy to three faiths. What had been essentially a conflict between nations is in danger of becoming a religious conflict, as well. In this case, dialogue could help to disentangle the so-called civilizational and religious questions from the political and territorial, so as to find answers and compromises that would honor all faiths by choosing a just peace over an interminable war.

I do not mean to suggest that there are not profound and very real issues of security, self-determination, and dignity at stake. But a dialogue of words and deeds – that is, of reciprocal actions based on a genuine appreciation for the other side's grievances – can make a difference in finding a path to lasting peace.

We want to reinvigorate the fight against intolerance – with legal measures, with education, with economic and social development. And we want to do so well before grievances and prejudice spiral out of control and people find themselves on the battlefield, in conflicts they neither want nor can afford to fight.

Intolerance around the world is as widespread as it is pernicious. But our challenge is not just to diagnose the disease. We must treat it. We cannot dismiss discrimination as an unavoidable aspect of human nature. Just as people can be taught to hate, so can they learn to treat others with dignity and respect. Nor can we accept intolerance as a predictable by-product of poverty, injustice, or poor governance. It is well within our power to change such conditions. Nor can we afford to ignore inflammatory rhetoric on the grounds that words can do little real harm. Hostile rhetoric is all too often the precursor to hostile acts, and hostile acts have a way of escalating into violence, conflict, and worse.

All of us need to join this battle. Governments can ensure that constitutional, legislative, and administrative guarantees are in place. They are also best placed to tackle the problems that fuel intolerance, such as unemployment. Presidents and prime ministers should lead the national dialogue on these issues.

Education, of course, has a central role to play. But education is not just a matter for schools. Some countries have taken special measures to integrate immigrant journalists into national and regional broadcasting enterprises. The business community can raise public awareness through its hiring and other practices. And education must begin at home; after all, that is where many racist attitudes have their origins.

There is a clear international dimension to this effort. United Nations treaties have often served as the basis for national laws. Our development work, peacekeeping operations, human rights programs, and humanitarian assistance all have the principle of equality at their core. Some of the most important work at the moment is being done by the International Criminal Tribunals for Rwanda and the former Yugoslavia. With recent convictions for genocide, rape, war crimes, and crimes against humanity, we are seeing important steps for accountability and against impunity.

Alongside the world's rich variety of civilizations, cultures, and groups, there is also, I believe, a global civilization that we are called on to defend and promote as we embark on a new century. It is a civilization defined by its insistence on universal human rights and freedoms, its tolerance of dissent, and its belief in the right of people everywhere to have a say in how they are governed. It is a civilization based on the belief that diversity is something to be celebrated, not feared. Indeed, many wars stem from people's fear of those who are different from themselves. Only through dialogue can such fears be overcome.

The United Nations, at its best, can be a forum where the dialogue among civilizations can flourish and bear fruit in every field of human endeavor. Indeed, one of the main lessons of the United Nations' first half-century is that without such a dialogue taking place every day, within and among all nations, no peace can be lasting, and no prosperity can be secure. If ever one doubted the need for a dialogue among civilizations, let them doubt no longer. September 11 made the need for such a dialogue crystal clear.

I am not saying that this dialogue will be easy. But we must not allow the difficulties we will face to deter us from pursuing it. I am convinced that it can make a genuine difference in the lives of ordinary men and women throughout the world. And that, ultimately, is the standard by which this dialogue will be measured – its ability to help alleviate suffering and protect the fundamental human rights of future generations.

The dialogue among civilizations has a purpose and promise beyond the challenges we face today. Such dialogue has throughout history fostered understanding and compromise, and can do so even more in a world that is ever smaller and more closely linked. It can support and sustain every effort at peace, and every attempt to resolve conflicts between and within nations.

It is my hope that in the months and years ahead all nations will join this dialogue, and make it genuinely valuable by placing it at the service of the weakest and most vulnerable of our world – the victims of intolerance, bigotry, and hatred. It is for their sake that the dialogue among civilizations must succeed.

15

The Productive Airing
of Grievances

Lord George Carey

Our world is in great peril. I am not reflecting on issues of the environment, or alarming poverty, or the world economy – each of which raises great debates about the future of our tiny planet. I am commenting, rather, on a sharp ideological tension that separates the West from another world, that we call "Islamic" and yet, as I shall presently show, does not reflect the true values of Islam. Just a short time ago I was in New York staying just two blocks away from the location of the former World Trade Center. It is impossible to visit it without feeling an enormous sense of sadness at the despicable events of September 11. But every American I spoke to was quite certain that, given the opportunity, other "Islamic" terrorists would wreak the same kind of punishment on the US. It is the association of the word "Islam" with terrorism that is the most disturbing feature of such assumptions. Yet, curiously, when one travels to the Middle East, a different assumption prevails. The West is identified with decadence, corruption, and materialism, and lack of faith.

Following the destruction of the World Trade Center, the *Financial Times* of February 27, 2002, arranged a unique public opinion poll that canvassed 10,000 people in nine Islamic countries: Saudi Arabia, Pakistan, Indonesia, Jordan, Morocco, Iran, Kuwait, Turkey, and Lebanon. The survey revealed populations deeply at odds with the West in general, and the United States in particular. The

United States was regarded as "ruthless, aggressive, conceited, arrogant, easily provoked and biased in its foreign policy." The respondents tended overwhelmingly to believe that "Western nations do not respect Arab or Islamic values; do not support Arab causes and do not exhibit fairness towards Arabs." Although the majority condemned the terrorist attack on September 11, significant minorities rejected the idea that Arabs, specifically Osama bin Laden's Al Qaeda network, carried out the attack. Significant numbers believed that Israel was behind it and was using it as a ploy to blame Arabs. Amazingly, a large number believed that the US engineered 9/11 for its own ends, but none of those canvassed indicated what might have been the US motive for so doing.

As far as the West is concerned, I do not have the fruits of a similar opinion poll to appeal to. What I do know from personal experience, gathered over many years, are the deep roots of Islamophobia. In Britain many assume that Muslims wish to take over "our" country, and that if we allow them to enter in significant numbers, they will in time make the country Islamic. To dismiss such worries as nonsense does nothing to remove such fears, because they are as firmly grounded in the minds of many in the West as are fears by many Muslims that a secular West is determined ruthlessly to pursue its own interests through globalization and destroy what they see as the true values of their societies by Western culture and media.

Clearly, then, we are dealing with similar worries, fantasies, and fears; clearly we are dealing with racial memories of bitter conflict and unresolved quarrels; clearly we are dealing with the baggage of the past.

First, from the Muslim side there is great resentment and anger at what is seen as the hypocrisy and deceit of the West in its opposition to Arab and Muslim cultures and religion. From a Christian point of view it is dispiriting that Western values are judged in this way, because the West owes more than it realizes to Christian values and its moral tradition. There can be little question that such values, shaped by the gospel of Jesus Christ, were at the heart of Western nations for hundreds of years. Christians regret deeply that the decline in religious observance has left many of our fellow citizens bereft of a code that can stop the drip, drip, drip of cyn-

icism, hedonism, and selfishness that goes with rampant materialism. A Muslim friend, Dr Abdullah Robin, wrote to me in an open
letter, "uncertainty and doubt are the post-modern virtues of
Western culture and there is no moral compass in that." I largely
agree with that, although I would argue that critics should pay
attention to the fact that the vast majority of Western people,
whether religious or not, have honorable ideals and seek to live
good lives. As someone who visits America regularly, I have a high
regard for American people. In certain respects America is more
deeply Christian than Britain. They may well fall short of the
entire ethical standards of Christianity that other Christians hold,
but of their desire to build stable communities and live at peace
with others, there can be little doubt. Neither should we overlook
the great contribution America makes to development in all parts
of the world. Nonetheless, the West needs to be reminded that
affluence and materialism are in their own ways as great dangers
to the human spirit as are dire poverty and lack of basic goods. I
suggest that here is a substantial challenge that Muslims, Jews,
Hindus, Christians, and people of other faiths may respond to
together by showing that there are abiding values that transcend
us all.

A second grievance from the Muslim side that greeted a lecture
I gave at the Gregorian University in Rome was my identification
of democracy with freedom of belief and human rights. I asked:
Why the glaring absence of democratic governments in Muslim
lands, particularly in the Middle East?

But let us look more thoughtfully at the issue of democracy and
the values that this form of polity safeguards. Winston Churchill
said of democracy that "it was the worst system of government
except for all the others." Indeed, Churchill's earthy and honest
appraisal of democracy recognizes that it too can be subverted
and distorted, as Nazi Germany illustrates in its most appalling of
forms. There in Germany, one of the most advanced nations in the
world, Hitler, democratically elected to govern, destroyed it from
within to permit injustice and evil to reign. So, if I or others are
going to promote democracy, where true values might flourish and
where proper learning and science are maintained, I must argue
why it is inalienably in this soil that they grow. Why should I

blame the failure of Muslim countries on the lack of democracy when the evidence seems that Western governments, though democratically elected, do not often appear accountable to the electorate?

The answers to such questions are bound up in our understanding of democracy and to the distinction that Ronald Dworkin, one of America's most prominent philosophers and jurists, has drawn between "majoritarian" and "egalitarian" democracy.[1] He characterizes majoritarian democracy as the "tyranny of the majority." It is that form of government that makes decisions by arithmetical procedure. We may, for example, decide that a motorway should be put through a valley of outstanding beauty because the majority demands it. Such a philosophy, comments Dworkin, may deny the equality of all citizens, even if they are in a minority, before the law. Egalitarian democracy, on the other hand, recognizes the equality of all citizens and enshrines their rights in codes or constitutions to protect minorities from violation by majorities. To be sure, a minority cannot hold the rest to ransom simply because it is a minority with rights. Some issues defy simple solution and require a careful balancing of interests to secure the best possible outcome. In such disputed cases, the inalienable rights of individuals have to be weighed against the needs of society generally and other factors that come into the equation. However, the bottom line should always be values and principles that are the bedrock of a good society. As Pope John Paul II stated in 1991, "A democracy without values easily turns into open or thinly disguised totalitarianism."[2] It follows from this that how a society treats its minorities is a gauge of its claim to be a fair and just society. It is my clear conviction that democracy, for all its faults, is the best system of government for safeguarding human rights and securing education, health care, and social provisions for all. It remains my hope that more and more Muslim societies will in days to come embrace this form of political life and include women in the electoral franchise. Nevertheless, it remains true that Western critique of Muslim societies for being too closed and too authoritarian should be balanced by Muslim criticism of Western systems of government that, by putting such a premium on individual freedom and rights, individual responsibilities and corporate moral principles that make for healthy community living may be undermined. We need to pay more careful attention to each other, and I, for one, do not rule out the possibility that Muslim experience of democracy in days to come will influence Western forms.

A third grievance has to do with the unfairness of Western governments in their treatment of Arab nations. From a Muslim point of view, America's uncritical support of Israel outrages millions of people throughout the world. I am as emphatic as anybody in asserting the right of Israel to exist, to live at peace, and to have safe and secure borders. Christians honor a legacy of faith derived from Judaism and must stand shoulder to shoulder with Jews in resisting anti-Semitism. Israel has done an extraordinary job in rejuvenating the land and becoming in 50 short years a powerful nation in spite of modest numbers. But the last 50 years have not been kind to another great people in the same land and neighborhood. The Palestinian people have become a humiliated and downtrodden people, ignored and despised. They see the ease with which certain United Nations resolutions have been used by powerful Western nations and how others have been ignored. It seems to them that might is right after all. From 50 years of unfulfilled hopes and rejected rights an ungovernable anger has arisen that is central to our present crisis. Let us make no mistake about it, the plight of the Palestinian people is the emotional epicenter of our current troubles, and healing this deep wound will go a substantial way to creating a more peaceful world.

Let me now turn to grievances from the side of the West that fuel misunderstanding. Muslim leaders are not doing enough to stop the murderous activities of suicide bombers and other terrorists who do not discriminate between innocent people and the military. In the Alexandrian Declaration signed in January 2002 by Muslim, Jewish, and Christian faith leaders, which I had the honor of chairing with the Grand Imman of Al-Alzar, we stated that "killing innocents in the name of God is a desecration of his Holy Name and defames religion in the world." I remain unapologetic about appealing to Muslim leaders to condemn outright such actions and to go on condemning. British Muslims have condemned such acts unconditionally, and I am delighted by their unswerving declaration. The statements of Middle Eastern religious leaders have been more ambiguous and diluted, except for the expression of unconstrained hatred of Israel. Let me press this point more firmly. Religious teachers have a responsibility to attack the theological roots of such a terrible dogma. If Islamic leaders give support to a theology that suicide bombers are in actual fact martyrs, this not only lends strong theological endorsement to such military tactics but also discredits Islam worldwide.

A second grievance stems from a sense of injustice from non-Muslims who feel second-class citizens in Muslim countries. I have received many letters from Christians whose experience in Islamic countries has been that of victimization and lack of freedom of worship. Let me quote from just one letter by a person who, sadly, will not allow his name to be revealed because he fears reprisals: "I have had first-hand experience of the pressures under which Christian converts from Islam labour . . . and in all cases they suffer under such disabilities that they are obliged either to conceal their change of religion or else live in a non-Muslim country. If they remain (in my country of origin) and are known as apostates from Islam, they face a lifetime of persecution and harassment." That letter is far from uncommon. Human rights, quite properly claimed by Muslims and others in the West, require the same right to be accorded to minorities in Muslim lands. In referring recently to Saudi Arabia in a last address and asking for freedom for other faiths to worship publicly in the Kingdom, a prominent Saudi replied to say that "those who live in the Kingdom are allowed to practice their religion and worship in their private homes." Cannot Muslims see that this is insufficient? Christianity, Judaism, Hinduism, and other faiths are not private religions only; they are faiths which, as much as Islam, need public expression. Anything that denies this is an affront to these faiths and a blow to human rights. Christians who worship in Saudi Arabia behind closed doors can be, and have in fact been, prosecuted and punished. Saudi Arabia should think again and allow other faiths freedom to their adherents to gather for worship.

So, these are some of the grievances felt by both sides of this debate and clearly are the ingredients of a deepening dialogue and debate. How are we to pursue it and with what tools?

First, I believe we should draw upon insights from our scriptures and cultures, laced with respect and understanding. I have recently read Jacques Dupuis's wonderful book, *Christianity and the Religions*.[3] In it he challenges Christians to discover in the Bible those elements that make a strong case for inclusion and not separation. He shows how the Hebrew Scriptures, followed by the New Testament, outline God's compassion and love for those who appear to be outside the community of faith. He studies such concepts as "logos" and "wisdom," together with many passages of the Christian Bible that lead to a broader interpretation than most Christians and Churches have usually given. Standing firmly within the Catholic tradition, Dupuis shows how it is possible to be orthodox in doctrine, yet receive other truths and insights from faiths other than our own. I suggest that this presents a challenge for us all to embark upon a dialogue that seeks to find support from within our own teachings for the inclusion of others. Recognizing that each of us may well maintain that truth is primarily to be found in "my" religion, may we draw insights from our own faith that lend support for inclusion rather than exclusion? Does my faith say anything positive about other faiths? For myself I have often been drawn to Wilfred Cantwell Smith's dictum that "for Christians God is defined by Jesus Christ, but not confined to Jesus Christ." To use a Christian term, does "grace" exist outside my faith tradition? Without compromising our own commitment, is it possible for Muslims, Jews, Hindus, Sikhs, and members of other faiths to endorse this from different perspectives? For example, in the Holy Qur'an, Surah 5, 8, it is written: "Nearest to you in love wilt thou find those who say 'We are Christians' because amongst these are men devoted to learning and they are not ignorant." That appears to express a generosity of spirit that invites closer dialogue and understanding, or more humility and not a little listening to one another's story and journey.

I return to the point I made at the beginning: we live in perilous times and each of us has a role to play in creating conditions that lead to peace. There is a Canadian saying: "No one snowflake thinks it is responsible for the avalanche." Yet each individual is significant because, combined, we have the potential to make a difference. We too, where we are, must move beyond talk of tolerance to take practical steps to engage those who cannot tolerate tolerance, those who use religion for evil ends, and those who harm the good name of Islam or any other faith.

May God give us the vision to refute the despairing lines of Matthew Arnold, who wrote of being caught "between two worlds, one dead, the other powerless to be born."

We are not powerless. Together, we can bring to birth a world of which we can all be proud and where Roosevelt's four freedoms become a reality everywhere: freedom of speech, freedom of religion, freedom from want, and freedom from fear.

Notes

1 Ronald Dworkin, *Taking Rights Seriously* (Cambridge, MA: Harvard University Press, 1978).
2 *Centesimus Annus*, p. 46.
3 Jacques Dupuis, *Christianity and the Religions* (London: Darton, Longman and Todd, 2001).

16

All of Man's Troubles

Edward O. Wilson

Vercours (Jean Bruller) expressed the core dilemma of humanity succinctly in his 1953 allegory, *You Shall Know Them*, as follows: "All of man's troubles arise from the fact that we do not know what we are and do not agree what we want to be." This existential difficulty can be put another way that points to its possible solution. We are a chimera. All of man's troubles arise from the fact that our emotions are Paleolithic, our mind-set medieval, and our technoscientific culture consequently destabilizing. Modern civilizations are like those depicted in the *Star Trek* and *Star Wars* film series, whose adolescent-brained warlords fight one another endlessly with the weapons of gods.

In the more than slightly insane circumstance of the present era, we find global culture divided into three opposing perceptions of the human condition. The dominant of these hypotheses, exemplified by the Abrahamic religions, sees humanity as a creation of God, who guides us with sacred scriptures and the wisdom of ecclesiastical authorities. The second worldview is that of political behaviorism, beloved of the now rapidly fading Marxist–Leninist states. It says that the brain is largely a blank slate, and as a consequence the mind originates almost wholly as a product of learning within a culture that itself has been evolved by historical contingency. Because there is no "human nature," people can be molded to the ideal political and economic system – to wit, and as urged upon the world during most of the twentieth century, communism. This belief was put to the test, and after repeated economic catastrophes and tens of millions of deaths in a dozen dysfunctional states, is generally deemed a failure.

Both of these worldviews, God-centered religion and atheistic communism, are opposed by a third, radically different worldview, scientific humanism. Still held by only a tiny minority of the world's population, it considers man to be a biological species that evolved over millions of years in a biological world, acquiring high intelligence yet still guided by complex inherited emotions. Human nature, the collectivity of these emotions, is the deep heritage of evolution. It adapts us with exquisite precision to Paleolithic life in which humanity lived during more than 99 percent of its existence. It composes the behavioral part of what Darwin, in *The Descent of Man*, called the indelible stamp of our lowly origins. To understand biological human nature well, to discourse clearly concerning its history and interaction with our evolving culture, will help deliver us from the fever swamps of religious and blank-slate dogma. But it also imposes the onerous burden of choice required by self-understanding and intellectual freedom.

Religion divides, science unites. In particular, religious dogma amplifies global conflict, and humanism based on science offers the only sure way to ameliorate this malign effect.

How did such a divisive force of human nature come into existence? The answer is that for most of humanity's deep, genetic history, religious belief provided an advantage. It united the members of each tribe during life-and-death struggles with other tribes; it buoyed up its devotees with a sense of superiority; it sacralized the tribal laws and mores; it lent solemnity through sacred rites to the passages of life; and it comforted the afflicted. From all this it gave people an identity and purpose, and in most venues it promised some form or other of personal immortality.

The competitive edge provided by myth making and religious passion, many biologists have concluded, helped to spread genes during evolution that prescribe a propensity to acquire these psychological processes. The brain is programmed to adopt some form of religiosity, whether the dogma of a structured religion or its equivalent in secular ideology.

The positive impact of religion on human history has been immense. It has generated much of what is best in culture, including the ideals of altruism and public service. In history it laid the foundation of the arts. Creation myths were in a sense the beginning of science itself: they were the best the early scribes could do to explain the universe and human existence.

Yet the essentially tribal origin of religions renders them forever and dangerously divisive, a fundamental and intractable flaw that has persisted into our own time. Our gods, the true believer asserts, stand against your false idols; our purity of soul against your corruption; our true knowledge against your error. This discordance, whether expressed as hate or mere humanitarian forbearance, continues in spite of the manifest absurdity of the mythologies that underlie traditional religion. It does not matter to true believers in immortality, for example, that the very idea is impossible. They believe but cannot imagine what forever in paradise means: the first trillion trillion years, a mere beginning, will see the universe in which we exist, unless God chooses to obliterate it at Armageddon, die a natural death, followed by a sequence of millions of other universes that may be born to replace it, and die; and yet each earth-born mind goes on, dwelling in an astral paradise apart from universes – and all because in one infinitesimal instant of time, it had been saved by a personal decision to accept the tribal religion, while sadly those not so fortunate as to have made that decision languish in hell, or just cease to exist.

Believers in life after death do not see that the soul cannot be separated from the mind, and cannot live in timeless bliss. What is bliss but an emotional quality of mind? In any event, what is that mind going to do in even the first trillion years? It must operate on physiological time, in molecular events that range in duration from microseconds to hours, if it is to exist at all. The brain is a narrative machine, a processor of temporal events. As a consequence, human beings, like all organisms, are creatures of unceasing growth and change. Their lives are cycles blended into the cycles of Earth, with a beginning and an end. Change that, and you lose the essence and the very meaning of the individual.

It matters not to the militant faithful who promote crusades, jihads, and proselytism that the righteousness of their cause exists only in the minds of men. The gods are surrogates of their passion, and in the end they and their gods win only by superior wealth and force of arms. So it matters not to true believers that the competing creation myths, which define the core religions and generate the conflicts, do not accord with what humanity has learned of the creation of the real world. In the case of the Abrahamic religions, it fails to perturb fundamentalist believers that, judging from testimony of his prophets and scribes, God either knew nothing of the world beyond what they could find out on their own or chose not to tell. The Qur'an and sacred texts of Judaeo-Christianity speak only for the worldviews and customs of several archaic patriarchies in the parched Middle East.

It is a commonplace to say that science is just another way of knowing, a producer of a specialized kind of information. But science is not a belief system, nor is it just a specialized kind of knowledge. It is a combination of mental operations that has become increasingly the habit of educated peoples, a culture of illuminations created by a fortunate turn of history that yields the most effective way ever devised of learning about the material world. Scientific knowledge, derived from the methods of science, is what humanity knows with reasonable certainty about the universe, including the human brain and mind. Because it is instrumental and objective in origin, as well as transparent and replicable, it transcends cultural differences.

Of necessity science remains forever skeptical. Its true manifestation is to say of any important principle "This is the best we can manage now, although it may be wrong," and continue to say that until overwhelming evidence dictates otherwise. The true manifestation of sectarian religious belief is the exact opposite. It says, "This is the best there is because it comes from God, or the gods, and it must be right, regardless of seemingly contrary evidence." Science generally, including the natural and social sciences, has in the past two centuries expanded objective, cause-and-effect knowledge of the physical world and human condition vastly more than all other forms of inquiry in previous history.

Scientific knowledge doubles approximately every two decades. Its epic of discovery and application is a force that draws humanity together. Being secular, it can silence the intellectual claims of false secular ideologies such as Nazism and Marxism-Leninism. But it cannot so easily confront the errancies of religion, which satisfy instincts hard-wired into the human brain by genetic evolution. The first step toward religious belief is surrender; the first step toward scientific humanism is learning, and of sometimes difficult subjects. Religious conviction can be quickly installed in any child, but the acquisition of knowledge and skeptical reasoning essential to intellectual independence comes hard. Swift indoctrination in dogma gave the Darwinian edge in Paleolithic times; rationalism and proven knowledge give the edge today.

We evolved genetically to believe one thing, and evolved intellectually to discover something entirely different. That in a nutshell is the dilemma of the human condition. There is no immediate solution. It is hard to see how different religions rooted in tribalism and idiosyncratic mythologies can be reconciled. Humanity will, in the true nature of the world, nevertheless evolve to a solution. Living most of their time in the real world on the near side of metaphysics, the vast majority of people desire the same things: peace, physical well-being, dignity, a family, a decent quality of life, some freedom of choice, an interesting and pleasant environment, the opportunity to improve their lot. With luck they will achieve those ends. There are favorable signs. The world population growth rate is falling, and is expected to peak under 10 billion by the end of the century. It has come to pass that when women gain some measure of personal independence, they choose to produce a small number of quality children over a large brood whose number diminishes the opportunities of each. Globalization of knowledge, not just of the economy, is accelerating. The more fantastical mythic beliefs are growing harder to swallow by all but the ignorant, and pragmatic moderates in public life stand a better chance as time goes on. The naturalistic worldview, based on science, is spreading in influence and will secularize the foundations of moral reasoning: tragic conflicts make it clear that religious dogmas are no longer adequate guides. There are a great many ways other than competing dogmas to satisfy tribal pride and the longing for purpose greater than self; and humanity will as a whole, I suggest, eventually settle upon those that are both global and irenic.

17

Turning Enemies into Friends

Jonathan Sacks

Twenty centuries ago, Judaism's sages posed the question: Who is a hero? In most literatures until recent times, a hero was one who performed mighty deeds on the battlefield, who fought, killed, and perhaps died in a noble cause. A hero is one who defeats his enemies. The rabbis thought otherwise. *Who is a hero? One who turns an enemy into a friend.*

I find that answer profoundly wise. If I defeat you, I win and you lose. But in truth, I also lose, because by diminishing you, I diminish myself. But if, in a moment of truth, I forgive you and you forgive me, then forgiveness leads to reconciliation. Reconciliation leads to friendship. And in friendship, instead of fighting one another, we can fight together the problems we share: poverty, hunger, starvation, disease, violence, injustice, and all the other injuries that still scar the face of our world. You gain, I gain, and all those with whom we are associated gain as well. We gain economically, politically, but above all spiritually. My world has become bigger because it now includes you. Who is a hero? One who turns an enemy into a friend.

How different the world would look if that idea prevailed. In the summer of 1999 I stood in the streets of Pristina, in Kosovo, amidst the wreckage of war. The NATO operation had just come to an end. The Kosovan Albanians had returned home. But in the air there was an atmosphere of bitterness and anger. Months earlier, the Albanians were in terror of the Serbs. Now the Serbs feared reprisals from the Albanians. There was peace, but not real peace. War had ended, but reconciliation had not begun. Many of the soldiers with whom I spoke feared for the future. They thought that some day – perhaps not tomorrow, not next year, but sometime – the conflict would begin again, as it has so often in that part of the world.

It was there, surrounded by broken buildings and broken lives, that I understood how one word has the power to change the world: *forgiveness*. If we can forgive others, and act so that others can forgive us, then we can live with the past without being held prisoner by the past. But only if we forgive. Without that we condemn ourselves and our children to fight old battles again and again, with the same bloodshed, the same destruction, the same waste of the human spirit, the same devastation of God's world.

Breaking the cycle is anything but easy. War needs *physical* courage. Reconciliation demands *moral* courage, and that is far more rare. In war, ordinary people become heroes. In pursuit of peace, even great leaders are afraid to take the risk. The late Anwar Sadat and Yitzhak Rabin had the courage to take that risk, and both paid for it with their lives.

Yet if humanity is to survive the twenty-first century, there is no other way. Our capacity for destruction has grown too large. Our ability to use new communications technologies to transmit hate has grown too great. The time has passed when antagonisms were local, containable, limited in their reach. The primary beneficiary of globalization has been terror – anger felt in one place, translated into devastation in another. War is fought on a battlefield. Terror has no battlefield. It has become global. Though it can be contained by physical measures, ultimately it must be fought in the mind. In the short term, conflicts are won by weapons. In the long run, they are won by ideas.

Early in the Second World War the poet W. H. Auden said, "We must love one another or die." That may be too lofty a hope, but at the very least we must try to turn enemies into friends. We must turn the clash of civilizations into a conversation between civilizations. In this, the world's great faiths must take a lead.

Is Religion Primarily a Source of Conflict?

Most religions value peace. Why, then, have they so often been a source of conflict? The word "religion" comes from the Latin root meaning "to bind." Religions bind people to one another and to God. They form a "We" greater than the "I." They create, in other words, group identity. That is precisely their power today. The twentieth century was dominated by the politics of ideology. The twenty-first century will be dominated by the politics of identity, and when it comes to identity, people turn to religion, for it contains humanity's deepest answers to the questions: Who am I? Why am I here? Of which narrative am I a part? How then shall I live?

However, the very process of creating an "Us" involves creating a "Them" – the people *not like us*, the other, the outsider, the infidel, the unredeemed, those who stand outside the circle of salvation. That is why, at the very time they are involved in creating community *within* their borders, religions can create conflict *across* those borders. That is why they both heal and harm, mend and destroy.

The Hebrew Bible contains a fateful warning at the beginning of its story of mankind. The first two human children, Cain and Abel, bring an offering to God – the first recorded act of religious worship. That led to rivalry, which led to animosity, which led to fratricide. The implication is unmistakable. Religion is like fire. It warms, but it also burns, and we are the guardians of the flame.

The original Hebrew text of the story of Cain and Abel contains an extraordinary verse which, because of its fractured syntax, is impossible to translate. Standard English versions have something like the following:

> Cain said to his brother Abel, "Let's go out to the field." And while they were in the field, Cain attacked his brother Abel and killed him. (Genesis 4: 8)

However, the words, "Let's go out to the field" are not in the original text. Literally translated, the text reads:

Cain said to his brother Abel . . . And while they were in the field,
Cain attacked his brother Abel and killed him.

"Cain said," but we do not discover what he said. The sentence
breaks off midway. Words fail. Conversation ceases. The dialogue
is interrupted. The two brothers can no longer speak to one
another. In this subtle but unmistakable way the Bible is signal-
ing one of its most fundamental truths. *When words fail, violence
begins.*

It is a point the Bible makes more than once. It happens in the
case of Joseph, Jacob's favorite son:

When his brothers saw that their father loved him more than any
of them, they hated him and could not speak a friendly word to
him. (Genesis 37: 4)

Their animosity festered. At one stage, the brothers thought of
murdering Joseph. Eventually they sold him into slavery.

Centuries later, King David's son Absalom discovers that his
half-brother Amnon has raped his sister Tamar. At the time, he
said nothing:

Absalom did not utter a word to Amnon, either good or bad; he
hated Amnon because he had violated his sister Tamar. (2 Samuel
13: 22)

This was the silence not of forgiveness but of cold calculation.
Two years later, Absalom took revenge.

In the case of Joseph, the biblical text contains another nuance
lost in translation. The Hebrew phrase translated as "they hated
him and could not speak a friendly word to him" literally means
"they could not *speak him to peace.*" As in the case of Cain and
Abel, syntactic awkwardness signals a powerful message. Communication is our greatest tool of conflict resolution. If hostility
is not discharged through dialogue, it will not disappear. Instead,
it will grow. Speech leads to peace if we can keep the conversation going, not allowing it to falter or break down under the pressure of strong emotion. Pain expressed, listened to, heeded, can be

resolved. Pain unheard and unheeded, eventually explodes. In the process, lives are lost.

Conversation as Prayer

The Babylonian Talmud (*Berakhot* 26b) contains a phrase (*Ein sichah ela tefillah*) which literally means, "Conversation is a form of prayer." This is a radical idea. In conversation I open myself up to an other. Speaking, I give voice to my hopes and fears. Listening, I hear another self and momentarily experience the world from a different perspective. Through encountering the human other, I learn what it is to encounter the Divine Other, the ultimate reality beyond the self. Prayer is an act not only of speaking but also of listening. Conversation is a form of prayer. In the give-and-take of speech lies the heart of our humanity. Genesis 2: 7 states: "And the Lord God formed man from the dust of the earth and breathed into his nostrils the breath of life, and man became a living being." An ancient translation reads the last phrase as "and man became *a speaking soul.*" Speaking is what makes us human. The human body is a mix of chemicals structured by DNA, what the Bible calls "dust of the earth." It is the use of language that infuses the body with the "breath of God." The highest definition of *Homo sapiens* is "the form of life that speaks."

It is often said that the Abrahamic faiths – Judaism, Christianity, and Islam – are the three great "religions of revelation." That is the wrong way to define their distinctiveness. *All* ancient faiths believed in revelation. They believed that the gods were to be found in phenomena of nature: the wind, the rain, the sun, the sea, the storm. What made the three Abrahamic monotheisms different is not that they believed that God reveals himself, but rather that he does so in *words.* They believe that *language is holy.*

Forces of nature signify power. Words signify meaning. Nature is indifferent to mankind. Language is the unique possession of mankind. What makes Judaism, Christianity, and Islam different from other faiths is that they conceive of God as personal, and the mark of the personal is that *God speaks.* Language is the only thing that spans the metaphysical abyss between one center of consciousness and another. It redeems our solitude, affirming that in the vast echoing universe we are not alone.

Therefore, to be true to our relationship with God, Jews, Christians, and Muslims must show that speech is greater than power, conversation more compelling than the use of force. God has taught us to listen to him for a reason: to teach us to listen to the other, the human other who, though not in our image, is nonetheless in his.

From Conflict and Violence to Reconciliation and Peace

Beginning in the sixteenth century, Europe embarked on a long process generally known as secularization. First science, then knowledge generally, then politics and power, and finally culture, sought and gained their independence from religion. Thus were born the secular university, the secular nation-state, and secular society.

The conventional wisdom is that these things happened because people stopped believing in God. In fact, it was not so. They happened because good, thoughtful, and reasonable people came to the conclusion that *people of God could not live peaceably with one another*. It was not God who failed but those who claimed to be his representatives on earth.

The closest analogy to the new international disorder of the twenty-first century is the age – the sixteenth and seventeenth centuries – of the great European wars of religion. Two stark choices lie ahead of us. Either religions will continue to be a source of conflict, in which case, after long and bloody battles, the world will be re-secularized, or religions will rise to the challenge. I have suggested that this challenge was implicit in the Abrahamic monotheisms from the very outset. The task God set and continues to set us was not to conquer and convert the world. That is the language of imperialism, not religious faith. It is to listen to the human other as if the Divine Other were speaking to us through him or her. I do not claim that this is easy. I do claim that it is necessary.

I am a Jew, and as a Jew, I carry with me the tears and sufferings of my grandparents, and theirs, through the generations. The story of my people is the story of a thousand years of exiles and expulsions, persecutions and pogroms, beginning with the First Crusade and culminating in the murder of two-thirds of Europe's Jews. For centuries, Jews knew that they, or their children, risked being murdered simply because they were Jews. How can I let go of that pain when it is written into my very soul?

Yet, for the sake of my children I must. Will I bring one victim of the Holocaust back to life by hating Germans? Does loving God more entitle me to love other people less? If I ask God to forgive me, does he not ask me to forgive others? The duty I owe my ancestors who died because of their faith is to build a world in which people no longer die because of their faith. I honor the past by learning from it, by refusing to add pain to pain, grief to grief. That is why we must answer hatred with love, violence with peace, and conflict with reconciliation.

Today God has given us no choice. There was a time when our ancestors lived surrounded by people who were like them. They could afford to say, "We are right. The rest of the world is wrong." We are no longer in that situation. We live consciously in the presence of difference. Our lives, our safety, our environment, our very future, are bound up with countries far away and cultures unlike our own. God has brought us eyeball to eyeball with the complex interdependence of his world, and now he is asking us: Can we recognize God's image in someone who is not in our image? Can you discern my unity in your diversity?

It took the death of 6 million people to bring Jews and Christians together in mutual dignity and respect. How many more people will have to die in the Middle East, Kashmir, Northern Ireland, the Balkans, before we understand that there are many faiths but God has given us only one world in which to live together. The time has come for us to replace the clash of civilizations with a respectful conversation between civilizations, and begin the hard but sacred task of turning enemies into friends.

18

Security through Dialogue

Queen Noor of Jordan

More than a decade has passed since Samuel Huntington first wrote about "the clash of civilizations" in his essay for *Foreign Affairs* in 1993. My husband, King Hussein, and I were in Washington in June of that year for our first state visit to the Clinton White House. The Persian Gulf War was over, but American air strikes against Iraq continued. I remember Secretary of State Warren Christopher telling the King during our visit that the United States had launched another missile attack against Iraq, this time against intelligence facilities in Baghdad, in retaliation for an alleged plot to assassinate former President Bush during a trip to Kuwait in April. Also that summer, an interim Oslo Accord was forged, to be followed by the Washington Declaration in 1994.

But peace for the Middle East, then and now, remained sadly elusive. As I recall my husband's decades of tireless efforts to break the impasse between the Palestinians and the Israelis, it was not the idea of a "clash of civilizations" that came most readily to mind to explain the setbacks, but the clash of political interests – indeed, the thicket of political clashes within the region, between America and the region and country to country – that created the obstacles to peace. And yet, as I watched the intensification of fighting among Croats, Muslims, and Serbs in the former Yugoslavia in those years, as I lamented the West's initial failure to support the Bosnian Muslims, I could not help but see the sectional fighting as a harbinger of vast and dangerous wars based on religious, tribal, and other cultural differences, the menacing clash of which Professor Huntington warned.

Today the phrase "clash of civilizations" has become a short-hand way of describing friction between the Islamic world and the West, a short cut to explain a complicated history and a multi-faceted conflict. To deny a cultural aspect to the differences between the Middle East and America, of course, would be plainly wrong; but to reduce the clash to simplistic formulations is to miss an important opportunity for the kind of deep understanding that would invite the first steps to rapprochement.

As someone with roots in both East and West, who has spent most of her adult life trying to build bridges between Arab and American culture, I have come to phrase the debate differently: not as a clash between Islam and Christianity, or between East and West, but between the forces of intolerance and the forces of understanding. In my work with the United Nations and human rights groups, I have time and again seen that the clashes that impede progress begin with individuals, political blocs, and even countries who insist that their way is the only way; who paint the world in black and white.

No one culture has a monopoly on either virtue or intolerance; such qualities are not apportioned geographically, or by religion. Advocates of compassion and peace can be found in all houses of worship. But a great gulf exists between those who are genuinely willing to listen to and empathize with others, and those who are not.

The greatest oppressors are those who feel entitled to impose by force their idea of what is right. The greatest injustices in human history occur when people believe so strongly in their own ideology that they are willing to hurt others in its name. The ideology can be one of self-preservation and lust for power, as with dictators. It can be paternalistic, viewing the oppression of women, emigrants, and the otherwise disenfranchised as "for their own good." Or it can be a so-called defensive policy that targets all dissent as a threat that must be dealt with preemptively. All of these arguments have been used in one way or another to justify injustice and conflict.

Because faith remains one of the most compelling wellsprings of human action, the justification for anarchy and nihilism is often cloaked in the language of religion. Today we have seen how the perverted actions of a violent fringe have hijacked the great faith of the prophet Muhammad for its own ends. Yet Islam has no monopoly on radical fundamentalism. Christianity has carried the banner of "Holy War" – not only at the time of the Crusades, but in recent years, in the bloody execution of "ethnic cleansing" in the Balkans. Tragically, there are also Jewish extremists who are willing to use violence to further their vision of a religious utopia; one of them killed Itzhak Rabin for daring to contemplate peace. Terrorist threats in America come far more frequently from Aryan rights fanatics spouting twisted Christian dogma than from Arabs or Muslims. But to single out a religion because it is used as a cover for evil is exactly the kind of black-and-white thinking that gives rein to the abuse in the first place.

To be sure, threats to all three Abrahamic religions, and others as well, are very real. Anti-Semitism is once more on the rise in Europe. Christians are subject to persecution in countries where they are in the minority, among them China, North Korea, Sudan, and Pakistan. And Muslims feel that their culture and faith are under attack in many places, especially in the current climate of fear and mistrust of Islam in the West in the aftermath of 9/11. It is convenient for many pundits to describe these affronts as a "clash of civilizations" and promulgate the view that nothing can be changed; that cultural differences are hard-wired; that no amount of dialogue will change the dynamic of conflict; and that geopolitical power politics, bolstered by the threat of force, is the only way to manage these crises.

My approach is quite another. Moderates of all creeds must embrace their shared, universal values, and defy those who cloak hatred in religious rhetoric. We must not let the idea of "a clash of civilization" become a self-fulfilling prophecy, heightening the fears of people who think in black and white. Unfortunately, news reporting that unfairly emphasizes Muslim violence feeds the human desire for simple explanations and even encourages pernicious conspiracy theories and the naming of scapegoats.

What has been lost in the seemingly endless news reports on so-called Islamist violence is that Islam itself is not inherently violent, intolerant, or closed-minded. The Qur'an prohibits violence except in self-defense: "Allah loves not the aggressors" and "let there be no hostility except to those who practice oppression." It acknowledges its kinship with the other great monotheistic religions, Judaism and Christianity, whose followers it calls the "People of the Book." Islam recognizes their shared origin, but also their diversity, and calls upon believers to value other cultures: "O mankind! We created you from a single (pair) of a male and a female, and made you into nations and tribes, that ye may know each other (not that ye may despise each other)."

Founded on such injunctions towards tolerance and equality, early Islam was a wellspring of human rights at a time when they were almost unknown in human institutions. There was remarkable freedom of religious worship throughout the Muslim world during its early expansion. And few Westerners realize that seventh-century Islam granted women political, legal, and social rights then unheard of in the West, rights, in fact, that women in the US and elsewhere still struggled for in the twentieth century. Early Islam based these new rights, such as the equal right to education, to own and inherit property, to conduct business, and not to be coerced into marriage, on the equality of men and women before God – this when the rest of the world considered women chattels.

Even in the conduct of war, Islam taught tolerance remarkable for its time. The Holy Qur'an and the Prophet Muhammad both explicitly called for combat to be conducted with honor, charity, and justice. Islam called for treating prisoners in a dignified manner, providing them with adequate food and clothing, and after the cessation of warfare setting them free – rights that even today are not always accorded to "enemy combatants" in the West. Generations of schoolchildren learn these principles through the words of the Prophet's first successor, Abu Bakr: "Do not betray, do not deceive, do not bludgeon and maim, do not kill a child, nor a woman, nor an old man," he instructed. "Do not burn; do not cut down a fruit tree. . . . if you come across communities who have consecrated themselves to the [Christian church], leave them."

Similarly, those who currently argue that Islam is somehow inimical to democracy need to examine it more closely, as have scholars like Abdul Karim Soroush. Islam practices traditions of *ijtihad* (interpretation), *ijma* (consensus), and *shura* (consultation). Decision making, through the process of *shura*, belongs to the community as a whole. Thus, the democratic values of political pluralism and tolerance are inherently compatible with Islam. Let us not confuse fundamental with fundamentalist. The test comes when one's principles appear to conflict with the rights and needs of others. It is one thing to be willing to die for one's beliefs, but quite another to be willing to kill for them.

Unfortunately, intolerance is easier than reason, a comfort to those who feel threatened, be they prosperous Westerners with much to lose or impoverished refugees with nothing. Whether practiced by a Middle Eastern dictator or a Western politician, blaming hated outsiders is the classic technique for distracting the populace from internal problems. When tensions become heightened, even moderates – seeing what they perceive as closed minds and an unwillingness to understand – can become polarized, driven away from the center and toward the extremes.

Extremism also grows from frustration, anger, and despair. People who feel they have nothing left to lose can resort to desperate acts. From long experience, I know that the majority in our region long for freedom and control over their own destinies. Two and a quarter centuries ago, a group of freedom fighters waged a war for "life, liberty and the pursuit of happiness." The people of the Middle East want and deserve no less. For them, as for people everywhere, true security derives from a sense of freedom, hope, and opportunity. That security is the ultimate source of peace.

Such security can be achieved, I believe, through three interrelated solutions: education, dialogue, and action. Important new reports have recently been released highlighting aspects of these issues as they relate to security and Arab–Western relations from multiple perspectives. One, the *Arab Human Development Report 2003: Building a Knowledge Society*, the second in a series written by a group of prominent Arab scholars and thinkers, explores how the people of the region can assume more responsibility for solving their own problems. After the first report, in 2002, underscored the cardinal obstacles to human development across the region – limitations in freedom, women's rights, and knowledge – the 2003 report examined in depth the critical need for knowledge. The other 2003 document, *Changing Minds, Winning Peace*, is a US government report on the importance of public diplomacy in the quest for security. One emphasizes the need for Arab nations to expand their access to knowledge and information, the other concentrates on the need for the United States to expand its efforts to communicate with – and, I would stress, listen to – Arabs and Muslims.

Both reports emphasize that there is a serious knowledge and communication gap between East and West, and to bridge that gap, each side must strive to educate itself and reach out to communicate with the other. Education is supremely powerful, more powerful in the long term, perhaps, than weapons. In the first place it provides people with the techniques they need to operate in an increasingly complex environment. It benefits us all by developing the modern world's most precious resource, the human mind. But more important, education can be the most effective tool for increasing global security.

In light of the history of foreign interference in the region, from the Crusades through colonialism and beyond, Arabs and Muslims in general mistrust Western motives. Some 80 percent, however, still admire Western educational methods, research, and technology. American-affiliated institutions in the Middle East provide a model not only of Western teaching methods, but of transparency, pluralism, and democratic practice – inspiring and admired political ideals that the Arab human development report hopes will take root in the region. And exchange programs and scholarships in the US show a constructive impact on opinions in the region that far outweighs their cost. Worldwide, some 200 current and former heads of state and 1,500 cabinet-level ministers, have been involved in American exchange programs, the single most effective means to improve attitudes towards the West, according to the public diplomacy report. Islam places the highest value on learning, a fact that has been obscured by sensational news stories about terrorist training camps masquerading as "madrasses." Education in the Golden Age of Islam, 1,000 years ago, emphasized independent, creative, analytical thinking, linked to the larger world – and planted the seeds of Western liberal education. The Islamic reverence for scholarship transmitted and enhanced new ideas from the East, ranging from mathematics, to music, to medicine. Islam spread enlightenment, justice and equity, intellectual creativity and the concept of a humane society, and through the preservation of knowledge helped bring about the end of a dark age in European history. Twelfth-century rationalist Islamic philosophers like Alfarabi, Avicenna (Ibn Sina) and Averroës (Ibn Rushd) prefigured the Enlightenment that gave rise to Western political systems. Today a renaissance of this kind of enlightened, broad-minded education can nurture the security we all seek.

Peace-centered education can give people the ability to open their minds, to ask the right questions, to look at the world from others' points of view. It can give them the skills they need to make their voices heard, without resorting to violence.

In our region, I have seen the bitter enmity of previous generations overcome, transcended by young people encouraged to meet and interact in an atmosphere of trust. Seeds of Peace, for example, founded after the first World Trade Center bombing in 1993, brings together youth from conflict-torn regions to break down the barriers of ignorance and prejudice. For a time, they live together and work to build mutual understanding and respect, to value communication over confrontation. When they go home, they continue to hold out their hands and hearts to each other. Even now – especially now – Seeds graduates phone or e-mail across conflict lines to comfort their friends in the midst of the worst violence their region has seen. They also inspire their families and neighbors to take a chance on hope and humanity. They have stared hatred in the face and refused to succumb. They are living proof that people can love their own country and also love their neighbors.

The movement towards peace education is growing. More than 100 US colleges and universities now have programs in conflict resolution. Internationally, groups as varied as the prestigious UNESCO Prize for Peace Education, now in its twenty-fourth year, and the affiliated Peace Education Network, as well as smaller, private initiatives such as The Global Leadership Academy and the Coexistence Initiative, are working to bridge the divides of longstanding violence. Internet-based programs such as BosnianKidsOnline and Eye-to-Eye, a web site for and by children in Palestinian refugee camps, are taking advantage of modern communications technology to break through the physical and psychological barriers on which conflict is built. There are a wealth of other programs I have worked with, from the United World Colleges network, to the McGill Middle East Program in Civil Society and Peace Building, to the United Nations International Leadership Academy in Amman, all predicated on the idea that bringing people of different backgrounds together to talk, listen, and learn is the surest route to tolerance and peace. Peace grows not only from goodwill and understanding, important as those are, but from the concrete results I have seen these programs produce, by motivated people pooling their ideas and resources in networks and forming creative coalitions to solve real problems in their own communities, across their countries, regions, and the globe.

This kind of education for peace, and indeed peace itself, is impossible without respectful dialogue based on genuine listening. Dialogue, rather than a debate that one side must win, or an inflexible exchange of entrenched positions, allows the voices of tolerance to be heard above the rhetoric of a "clash."

Recent examples prove that this is not only possible, but productive. Many people are taking courageous steps to support such dialogue. The Geneva Accord drafted in November 2003 was the fruit of cooperation between people exhausted by violence and political stalemate in the Middle East who dared to defy the inflexible extremism of their own party leadership and had the moral courage to compromise. As one of the Accord's architects, former Palestinian Information Minister Yasser Abed Rabbo, put it: "Today we are extending our hands in peace for peace. Our critics say that officials should make such agreements, not representatives of civil society. We could not agree more," he said. "But what do we do if officials do not meet, if governments do not negotiate? We cannot wait and watch as the future of our two nations slides deeper into catastrophe."

King Hussein, one of the world's senior statesmen and a driving force behind a wealth of peace treaties, inspired the different people of the region to understand what he believed so deeply, that peace is made not among governments, but among people; it is not only written on pieces of paper, but must be enshrined in the hearts of those who live together side by side, who sacrifice for and sustain real peace.

This Accord is the epitome of that idea. Fifty-eight former presidents, prime ministers, foreign ministers, and other global leaders have voiced their support, but, more important, a majority of Palestinians and Israelis, weary of waiting for their leaders to make peace, agree with its principles. Although it is not politically binding, the Accord demonstrates the power of civil society to act as a catalyst for breaking the stalemate and building consensus.

Other civil groups are crossing conflict lines as well. Women Waging Peace has formed a network of peace-builders who use the power of modern technology and women's unique perspectives to cut across political and doctrinal boundaries and help ravaged communities recover from conflict.

In Guatemala, where the Vision Guatemala project has begun, according to its founder, to "change the world by changing how we talk and listen"; in El Salvador, where the Culture of Peace radio program brings former factions together in dialogue; in the Philippines, where the organization Kusog Mindanão is reaching out to the Muslim minority; in the Balkans, where women on both sides of the conflict came together to mourn because "we are all mothers"; in Sierra Leone, where women have joined forces to help reintegrate former child combatants; and in many other places, men, women, and children are reaching out to talk, to listen, and to begin healing the scars of longstanding violence.

Above all, the premier example of dialogue across borders is the United Nations. Having worked in various forms of partnership with the UN for a quarter-century, addressing issues from hunger to the environment to refugees to children's welfare, and scores of others, I can attest that the UN, whatever its challenges today, is one of the most powerful engines for cooperation ever created by humankind. Founded on the principle that the world is a family of nations, it has demonstrated on repeated occasions that the strength of any family depends on ceaseless effort at communication.

Indeed, communication, not propaganda or glib public relations gestures, is the key to success. Such initiatives, no matter how worthy, flounder when their representatives try to convert others to their position through harsh and unyielding stances. But when organizations listen, try to find common ground, and – even when consensus cannot be found – respect differences, they open a dialogue that invites opportunity. This is a matter not only of goodwill, but of safety, for closing off the lines of communication out of fear – shutting down educational and cultural exchange programs, for instance, or restricting travel, burdening travelers, or making visas prohibitively difficult to obtain – only increases tension and misunderstanding. Sharing knowledge, education technology, and ideas across borders and cultures is absolutely vital to international security. Newly restrictive defensive security measures are directly and seriously harming the very security they seek to protect.

But there is one more crucial element in the fight against fanaticism, without which the other two count for little: action. The most powerful educational programs and the most intensive communications efforts will not change minds if actions make them look like lies. No amount of public diplomacy can assuage anger in the Middle East towards US and Western policies on the ground as long as the occupation of the Palestinian Territories continues. America's efforts to build cultural bridges to the Middle East will be held in suspicion as long as its soldiers occupy Iraq.

The core values of modern Western culture are tolerance, freedom, democracy, and human rights, but, tragically, many throughout the world see the United States and its allies abandoning, in the name of security, the very values they claim to protect. Certainly, those in positions of authority in the Middle East must do their utmost to curb the violence spawned by a fanatical minority in their midst, and to encourage the forces of moderation by opening up political and economic systems, safeguarding human rights, and giving sustainable development priority over military buildup. But the same must hold true for the other side of the so-called culture clash.

Security requires action as well as words. But that action cannot be unilateral and coercive. It must be mutual, positive, and cooperative. Recent events make it quite clear that successful international action is impossible without international cooperation. Besides the inevitable resentment that builds when one nation intervenes unilaterally in another, no nation, even the most powerful, can change the world alone. For reasons of morality, legitimacy, and practicality, global intervention must be based upon international norms and involve credible multilateral institutions – especially the UN.

The premise "If you're not with us, you're against us," when used as a basis for action, is a surefire way to incite conflict, whether it is delivered from a pulpit in a mosque or from a presidential podium.

It is hard to be a passionate moderate, but that is what we need now, in every culture. It is especially difficult because tolerance, by its very essence, cannot be imposed. Coercion is easier than persuasion. To take refuge in extremism and condemn others on the basis of half-truths and exaggerations is fairly simple. But to pay attention to nuance, especially the nuances of other cultures, and still be able to act decisively, is a delicate balancing act. Conviction and compassion *can* go hand in hand.

September 11, 2001, was supposed to mark the celebration of the International Day of Peace at the UN, a highlight of the Year of Dialogue among Civilizations. Instead, history itself was hijacked by the forces of intolerance. The fanaticism of a few destroyed the lives of thousands – citizens of 70 nations, including more than 200 Muslims. When the voices of extremism and hatred drown those of moderation, everyone suffers, not any one culture or creed.

We are not facing a new clash of civilizations. We are seeing civilization in its age-old struggle against inhumanity. Fanaticism has always bedeviled mankind, but we cannot abandon mankind because of it. Neither can we wrap ourselves in a comforting blanket of dogma, to keep us from facing the hard questions. Through education, communication, and action, those who believe in tolerance, compassion, and the rights of others can join forces to reinforce the global community of shared benefits, responsibilities, and values.

It has been said that there are two kinds of people in the world: those who divide people into two types, and those who don't. This aphorism has more than a grain of truth: It is so much easier to divide the world into us versus them than to praise the richness of its diversity. But it is in the glory of diversity that true dialogue among civilizations is forged.

19

The Power of Dialogue: Redefining "Us"

Tamara Sonn

The concept of interfaith dialogue developed in the aftermath of the Holocaust. Building on momentum that had developed among people of conscience throughout the world, the Second Vatican Council (1962–5) of the Roman Catholic Church articulated the rationale for dialogue and gave it structure. The Church had recognized the negative effects of traditional Christian exclusivism. At best, it had resulted in isolation and a lack of social engagement. At worst, Christian exclusivism had manifested itself in contempt for other faith communities and genocidal attacks. To address the former issue, Vatican II's "preferential option for the poor" encouraged active intervention in the socioeconomic and political structures that lay at the root of human suffering. Regarding the latter, the Church's new "ecumenism" encouraged dialogue as an effort to bridge the gaps of understanding among various religious communities.

During its first few decades, dialogue took on a life of its own, independent of the broader goals envisioned by those inspired by the lessons of the Holocaust. Centuries of inertia had to be overcome, along with generations of misinformation, misunderstanding, and suspicion among various faith communities. Early dialogues often turned on simple clarification of beliefs and practices. As well, partners had to be identified, and procedures and guidelines developed, as interfaith encounters occasionally degenerated into arguments over which interpretations were accurate. At the same time, religious foundations had to be scrutinized, both to find ways to legitimate the dialogue effort in the first place and to respond to issues raised during interfaith encounters.

In these early years, the progress of dialogue efforts often seemed slow, but the true potential of dialogue is now becoming clear. Dialogue has matured from initial efforts at self-disclosure and mutual toleration. It is now rejoining the broader social efforts in which it was born. In the process, it is forging new communities, communities made up of people of diverse backgrounds working together to expunge the roots of suffering that lie in communal exclusivism. These new communities do not replace traditional religious communities. Instead, they bring together people who may differ in communal identities, but who nonetheless share common values. In so doing, they actually strengthen the communities of all the participants. Shifting the focus of discourse from articles of faith to shared socio-moral concerns, contemporary dialogue is creating coalitions of people determined to transcend the barriers of traditional group identity, and to work together to resolve longstanding conflicts in which all sides suffer.

The Ahmed–Pearl Dialogues

Among the best examples of this kind of dialogue is one that grew out of shared grief over the murder of innocents by terrorists. That was the origin of a series of dialogues, ongoing as of this writing, between Judea Pearl – the father of slain *Wall Street Journal* reporter Daniel Pearl – and renowned Islamic scholar and diplomat Akbar Ahmed. Danny Pearl was executed by terrorists in Pakistan in early 2002, in a grotesque spectacle made public through video footage on the internet. His final words were, "I am Jewish." Struggling with immeasurable grief, his parents sought revenge – but not the kind that is at the basis of the cycle of violence we see in the Middle East and elsewhere. "I seek a symbolic form of revenge," said Dr Pearl during his dialogue with Dr Ahmed at the College of William & Mary in April 2004. His goal is to understand the roots of the hatred that killed his son, as it has killed so many others, and find ways to overcome it.

As a first step, Dr Pearl sought out Dr Ahmed, whose book *Islam under Siege: Living Honorably in a Post-Honor World*, had struck a chord with him. Two things particularly impressed him. First, he said that as a Jew growing up in Israel in the wake of the Holocaust, it had never crossed his mind that Muslims also feel threatened. In *Islam under Siege*, Dr Ahmed lays out the narrative that dominates modern Islamic discourse. That discourse traces the Christian West's attacks against Muslims, beginning with the Crusades, following through the efforts of missionaries and colonial powers, and culminating in the current scenario of Muslims under attack in Bosnia, Palestine, Iraq, Afghanistan, Kashmir, and Chechnya. The words of American Protestant religious leaders decrying Islam and the Prophet Muhammad serve as evidence to many that there is now not just prejudice against Muslims but a concerted effort to destroy Islam itself. This perception was a revelation to Dr Pearl. "What I've learned is that Muslims feel genuinely under siege," he said during the discussion at William & Mary. At least as important to Dr Pearl was Dr Ahmed's recognition that Jews feel threatened. "In Israel we are under the threat of constant annihilation," Dr Pearl continued, but he had never seen a Muslim acknowledge this perception before reading *Islam under Siege*. It was this that prompted him to contact Dr Ahmed.

At the William & Mary dialogue, the third in the series, the power of contemporary dialogue became apparent. The discussion began with the shared history of Jews and Muslims. "Here are two Abrahamic peoples in the Middle East," said Dr Ahmed. "Some verses in the Torah and the Qur'an are identical." But the focus of this dialogue was not on doctrinal issues or the authenticity of various traditions. The discussion was dominated by concerns about ending the cycle of violence, overcoming hostilities between groups traditionally considered enemies, and establishing a framework in which all those determined to leave a peaceful legacy to the next generation could work.

The discussants did not always agree, nor did they shy away from difficult issues – the war in Iraq, for example. Dr Ahmed placed the blame for the current turmoil on what he characterized as hasty and emotional reactions to the terrorist attacks of September 11. Dr Pearl responded that he believed America had no choice but to respond to the attacks with violence. While America was obliged to react to the attacks, Dr Ahmed countered, the nature of the reaction was, and continues to be, counterproductive. "Every time you drop a bomb, you are helping Osama bin Laden," he said. Drs Ahmed and Pearl did agree, however, that Muslim leaders must commit themselves to education in order to eradicate the roots of hatred and violence, and that the international community must assist in that effort. "We need to help Muslims see the other side," said Dr Pearl. Dr Ahmed agreed, adding that the media must assist as well. The media, recognizing their responsibility as educators and image-makers, in addition to being news broadcasters, must avoid filling the airwaves with negative images that can serve as both stereotypes and role models, and focus as well on positive elements.

Dr Pearl brought up one such positive development. He said he had recently received a letter from an organization called World Tolerance Fund. The letter included pictures of Pakistani children lighting candles in commemoration of Danny Pearl. "Above the picture of my son was a sign reading: 'Peace through dialogue, discussion, and debate.' " Contrary to the perceptions of people who think that terrorists represent Islamic values, Dr Ahmed pointed out that these children are motivated by a respect for the value of human life, a value shared by all monotheists. The scriptures of Jews, Christians, and Muslims teach that the taking of an innocent life is tantamount to taking the life of all humankind, and the saving of a single life is like saving all humanity. The children's commemoration was, in effect, an Islamic rebellion against the values of the terrorists.

The dialogues between Dr Ahmed and Dr Pearl could also be included among the most positive developments of our age. In the very process of channeling his grief through efforts to root out the hatred that took his son's life, Dr Pearl is helping to break the cycle of violence. And in accepting the hand extended in the pursuit of peace, Dr Ahmed – like the Pakistani children in the photo – is demonstrating that the rifts between groups of people need not run along lines of religious or national identity.

The deeper conflicts are between people who respect human dignity and the rule of law and have the courage to confront violations of those values even when they are committed by members of their own communities, and those who do not.

Perhaps predictably, some have responded negatively to Dr Ahmed's and Dr Pearl's efforts. They ask what is so special about the death of Danny Pearl? They say that people are being killed every day – in the West Bank, Gaza, Iraq, Afghanistan – and no one seems to care. What is so special about Danny Pearl's death is the reaction to it. Dr Pearl and Dr Ahmed have rejected the age-old interpretation of vengeance. While "an eye for an eye" may have worked to maintain stability in the days of the Code of Hammurabi (where it was first articulated), the Hebrew Bible and the Qur'an (both of which repeat it), it is clear that in the modern world it does not. Both Ahmed and Pearl seek justice, but the justice they seek is a kind that prevents others from having to suffer the kind of loss that the Pearl family, like so many other families, has suffered. Dr Pearl and Dr Ahmed are demonstrating that people of clear vision and conscience, regardless of traditional religious or ethnic identities, can work together on the basis of shared values and commitment, for the benefit of all humanity. The opponents are not members of a single religious, national, or ethnic identity, but those who perpetuate hatred and vengeance.

Expanding the Power of Dialogue

The Ahmed–Pearl dialogues are not the only such efforts. Addressing the Palestinian–Israeli conflict alone, a number of initiatives are under way. For example, Seeds of Peace was founded in 1993 to bring Jewish, Christian, and Muslim children together for shared summer living experiences, during which regular dialogues are conducted. In sharing their hopes and concerns, participants learn that far more is to be gained by working together than in opposition. The project has been so successful that it has expanded its reach. It now brings children from various sides of other conflicts together, based on the model of conflict resolution through dialogue. The Israeli village called Oasis of Peace – "Neve

Shalom" in Hebrew and "Wahat al-Salam" in Arabic – was founded 25 years ago specifically to bring Jewish, Muslim, and Christian families together for similar purposes.

Dr Pearl himself took inspiration from the parents of Amy Biehl. Amy Biehl was a Stanford University graduate student working to improve the lives of South Africans struggling under the apartheid system, when she was murdered by some of the very people she was trying to help. Her parents faced a choice. They could let Amy's ideals die with her, or they could try to find a way to continue her work. They chose to sell their business and move to South Africa, where they established the Amy Biehl Foundation to carry their daughter's work forward in the same communities where their daughter was killed. As her father said, "The most important vehicle of reconciliation is open and honest dialogue. . . . We are here to reconcile a human life which was taken without an opportunity for dialogue." Dr Pearl faced the same choice. "My son Daniel was a dialogue-maker," he said. "He possessed an unshaken belief in using communication and education to change people's minds and hearts." The Pearl family established the Daniel Pearl Foundation to carry on this work. It now has an international board and supporters around the world. Through programs dedicated to education and music – another of Danny Pearl's means of communicating; he was an accomplished violinist – the foundation is carrying forward the dialogue to create community among people who have not lost faith in human decency, regardless of religion or nationality.

The long-term results of such efforts cannot be predicted. The weight of centuries of tradition and the burden of decades of conflict pose formidable obstacles to prospects for success in the struggle for peaceful conflict resolution. Nor does dialogue offer a quick fix or anything like the instant gratification offered by violent strikes of vengeance. The reaction of students participating in the William & Mary dialogues was instructive. Whether Jews, Christians, or Muslims, their overwhelming response was a sense of relief to know that there is hope, a way to break the seemingly endless cycle of violence that has characterized the Middle East throughout their lifetimes. But at the same time, they said the sense of hope was mixed with a feeling of enormous responsibility. Knowing that there is indeed a way out, they said, they felt they could not ignore it. They felt compelled to commit themselves to breaking out of their traditional "comfort zones," challenging well-worn prejudices and finding ways to inspire others to do the same. They had to reject the fleeting sense of communal belonging and embrace the insecurity of those who challenge the status quo. But they agreed that the challenge was worth the risk. The bravado displayed by warriors, as one student put it, only masks the despair of failure. Those who offer their lives in attacks against the innocent are already spiritually dead. The students said that the Ahmed–Pearl dialogue had shown them how to work with others to secure life.

Generations of people, numbed by daily mounting death tolls, have silently slipped into the margins, avoiding sociopolitical engagement and allowing the ideals of youth to be dismissed as romantic myths. The great gift offered by those engaged in dialogue is hope that this trend can be reversed, that the ideals of peace can indeed be achieved. In taking their dialogue to the public, Drs Ahmed and Pearl are, in fact, giving voice to the silent majority. They have shown others that they are not alone in rejecting hatred and violence, and can forge bonds with those of all faiths to resolve conflicts peacefully. This is the power of dialogue.

20

On Clash, Morality, Renaissance, and Dialogue

Judea Pearl

In his speech of April 15, 2004, President George Bush linked the murder of my son, Daniel Pearl, to a global "ideology of murder." "The terrorist who takes hostages, or plants a roadside bomb near Baghdad," said Bush, "is serving the same ideology of murder that kills innocent people on trains in Madrid, and murders children on buses in Jerusalem, and blows up a nightclub in Bali, and cuts the throat of a young reporter for being a Jew."

A week later, while engaging in a Jewish–Muslim dialogue in Williamsburg, Virginia, the first question reporters asked me was: "What is your reaction to the President's mention of your son?" My answer was: "I agree with the President's observation that Daniel's tragedy is pivotal for understanding the current tide of madness. However, I consider Danny's legacy as a communicator and bridge builder to be equally pivotal in inspiring and revitalizing East/West dialogues, an effort to which I am currently devoting most of my energies."

President Bush was right about this. The wave of violence now rocking the planet is of a fundamentally different character from anything this planet has ever known. For the first time in history, friendly messengers are killed by calculated design, in front of millions of spectators, for the sheer purpose of transmitting a message to those deemed enemies.

True, planet earth has known cruelty before, and on a much greater scale. Yet even the Nazis labored to hide their gruesome deeds, thus unveiling some inkling of shame, doubt, or fear. Daniel's murderers, in shocking contrast, boasted openly in their cruelty, totally secured in faith and righteousness, triumphantly expecting spectators to rally in sympathy. More shocking yet, many of their spectators did rally in sympathy (according to reports from Pakistan and Saudi Arabia), and, as the 2004 murders of Nicholas Berg and Fabrizio Quattrocchi indicate, message-transmission killing has become an increasingly acceptable practice in certain parts of the world.

Such brazen assault on the sanctity of human life marks a profound transgression in the evolution of human civilization, and we must ask ourselves what the origin of this transgression is, and whether it can be isolated, understood, and controlled.

I used to believe that, in its core, the current global conflict reflects a clash between two camps, one inclusive, embracing those who are respectful of differences among cultures and viewpoints, the other exclusive, for those intolerant of such differences. I had this distinction in mind when I wrote, "we must galvanize people along a new frontier, one defined not along national or religious lines but along lines of decency and understanding."[1]

But this inclusive/exclusive distinction (or compassionate versus judgmental, as it is sometimes called) is flawed with incurable contradictions – it cannot serve as the sole basis for moral judgment. The contradictions belong to a family of logical paradoxes investigated by Bertrand Russell in 1903 which is endemic to self-referential criteria.[2] Imagine a person who proclaims himself "inclusivist." Naturally, that person would view himself as part of the inclusive camp, to the exclusion of the opposite camp, comprised of exclusivists. But this very view is inherently exclusive, us versus them, which immediately puts that person back into the exclusive category, in blatant contradiction of our starting premise.

Russell's paradox cannot be brushed aside as an academic exercise in sophistry. Its power caught my attention in a pertinent discussion with a Pakistani friend who stated that he cannot stand people like President Bush who take an "us-versus-them" attitude.

I pointed out to my friend that by excluding himself from the us-versus-them camp he is in fact positioning himself in the very same camp that he loathes so intensely.

The lesson of Russell's paradox is that one simply cannot be inclusive all the way. Even the most accommodating and compassionate person must reject certain ideologies without losing the moral high ground we normally associate with tolerance, pluralism, and inclusivity. Examples of rejectable ideologies include those that advocate intolerance of different cultures and faiths, those that threaten the survival of mankind, and those that trample on basic norms of civilized society.

This paradox also presents a compelling argument against theories of relativistic morality, according to which right and wrong, good and evil, are in the eye of the beholder; a "terrorist" to one eye is a "freedom fighter" to another, "occupiers" to some are "liberators" to others, and so on. Such blurring of distinctions, a favorite occupation of post-modern media, has helped legitimize the ideology of bin Laden, and leads to moral bankruptcy everywhere.

These symmetries should be broken by reference to objective norms of right and wrong adopted by civilized society. There is simply no moral equivalence between those who labor to minimize the suffering of innocents and those who pride themselves on maximizing such suffering.

It is this reliance on absolute basic norms, not on the inclusive/exclusive distinction, that makes the perpetrators of the 9/11 attack, the killers of Daniel Pearl, and the sadists in Abu Ghraib prison morally repulsive, even to a world embroiled in ideological conflicts and moral confusion.

We must now ask ourselves what divides those capable of beheading people for the purpose of transmitting messages and those who are repulsed by such acts. Is the dividing line cultural? religious? ideological? political?

Samuel Huntington theorized that the dividing lines represent a clash among civilizations, most acutely between Muslim and Western. It is not a fashionable theory today among intellectuals, partly because it implies a long and irreconcilable struggle between two vast populations, and partly because it associates terrorism with religious or cultural backgrounds – a distasteful association at least by Western standards.

Pakistan's President Pervez Musharraf, on the other hand, has promoted an alternative theory, one that is often heard in the West from Muslim spokesmen:

> We need to understand that the root cause of extremism and militancy lies in political injustice, denial and deprivation. Political injustice to a nation or a people, when combined with stark poverty and illiteracy, makes for an explosive mix. It produces an acute sense of hopelessness and powerlessness. A nation suffering from these lethal ills is easily available for the propagation of militancy and the perpetration of extremist, terrorist acts.[3]

Although not mentioned explicitly, religion-based incitement was surely on Musharraf's mind when he talked about "explosive mix." One could hardly be oblivious to the fact that the "explosions," when they occurred, were made in the name of religion, and received the tacit approval of the religious leader who held the moral authority to safeguard against such explosions. Thus, the difference between Huntington's theory and those based on socioeconomical or political factors is merely a question of which factors we take as the fuel and which as the spark. These analogies have significant implications on the choice of effective strategies to tame the current conflict.

Musharraf's strategy, which he calls "Renaissance" and "Enlightened Moderation", goes as follows: "The first part is for the Muslim world to shun militancy and extremism and adopt the path of socioeconomic uplift. The second is for the West, and the United States in particular, to seek to resolve all political disputes with justice and to aid in the socioeconomic betterment of the deprived Muslim world."[4]

It is hard to disagree with the general outline of this strategy, though it requires two essential clarifications. First, as a member of the Jewish "Ummah" (nation), I hope that the equation for "justice" in the enlightened era would include the legitimate aspirations of non-Muslim nations as well, including aspirations for normalcy, self-determination, diplomatic recognition, and unqualified acceptance. Second, and most importantly, one must emphasize and explicate the essential role that spiritual Muslim leaders must play in this transition toward Enlightened Moderation.

Religions, civilizations, and ancient scriptures do not provide us with complete recipes for moral behavior. Rather, they provide us with intellectual resources or building blocks with which we construct criteria for evaluating actions in specific situations. One of the primary functions of spiritual and ideological leadership is to help us decide which cultural building blocks are applicable in any given situation, and filter out those that do not apply. An enlightened leadership is one that institutionalizes those filters to safeguard religion from being hijacked by its extreme elements; that is the kind of leadership that is absolutely needed for restoring enlightenment.

If we focus on ideological leadership as the guiding paradigm for understanding the current conflict between the Muslim and Western worlds, then the conflict, even considering its cultural-religious roots does not seem as hopeless as the one predicted by Huntington's theory. Ideological differences are a matter of emphasis, leaving scriptures and beliefs intact; they can be smoothed by renaissance and dialogue.

In the Muslim world, the leaders who can make renaissance a reality are those who can win the minds of the young and faithful to the side of hope: intellectual leaders who pride themselves on peace and modernity, and clerics, imams, sheikhs, and mullahs who have been voicing concern over the hijacking of Islam by a minority of anti-Islamic extremists. A first step in winning the minds of the young is for these leaders to articulate the distinction between true Islam and jihadi Islam in religious, not political, vocabulary.

A week after the brutal killing of Nicholas Berg I addressed Muslim leaders in an open letter:

> I beseech you to join the courageous Muslims who have denounced, in unambiguous language, not only the killing of Nicholas Berg, but the growing practice of killing innocent human beings as a means of communicating grievances, regardless of how valid or urgent the grievance . . . I therefore urge Muslim clerics to

cast their denunciation in plain religious vocabulary, to proclaim these crimes to be sins, or blasphemy, and to remind their followers that the murderers of Nicholas Berg, Fabrizio Quattrocchi and Daniel Pearl will be punished by Allah Himself, as it is said: 'We have prepared fire for the wrongdoers' (Qur'an: 16).[5]

Muslim clerics can further guard the image of Islam by issuing fatwas against the perpetrators of those acts, thus mobilizing their communities to take a pro-active role in the apprehension of those perpetrators, and in bringing them to justice.

The use of Islamic instruments such as "Haram," "Takfir," and "Fatwa" is essential in the transition to Musharraf's Enlightened Moderation. As Shmuel Bar notes in his June–July 2004 *Foreign Policy* article:

> The fatwas promulgated by sheikhs and 'ulama who stipulate that jihad is a 'personal duty' play, therefore, a pivotal role in encouraging radicalism and in building the support infrastructure for radicals within the traditional Islamic community. While one may find many fatwas which advocate various manifestations of terrorism, fatwas which rule that those who perform these acts do not go to paradise but inherit hell are few and far between.[6]

I am hopeful that these instruments, which Islam provides its spiritual leaders to protect its true teachings and which were abused by some to distort and defame its roots, will be used to create the conditions for Enlightened Moderation to emerge.

One reason for optimism stems from the presence of a sizable Muslim "diaspora" in the West. This diaspora can serve as a cultural conduit of ideas and needs from the West to the East, and vice versa. Although many Western Muslims feel alienated and express disenchantment with Western motives and values, they nevertheless have experienced the merits of Western freedoms and are fully aware of the genuine goodwill of their non-Muslim friends and neighbors. They could serve as the West's best ambassadors to their countries of origin, and vice versa.

More importantly, Western Muslims are serious victims of post-9/11 Islamophobia and of the distorted image of Islam that silence and lethargy are projecting. They have a vested interest in seeing that silence broken and enlightenment ensue. It is from the mosques of the West that a grassroots pressure for a cultural renaissance is likely to emerge and make its way eastward.

I envision a natural partnership developing between Muslims, Jews, and Christians in the West and slowly making its way, through religious channels, toward South Asia, the Middle East, and other Muslim countries. It is in building such partnership that dialogue among the three great religions plays a crucial role. Western Muslims must be assured that Jews and Christians are reliable supporters of their legitimate struggle for dignity and social acceptance. Jews and Christians, on the other hand, need to be assured that Western Muslims will become partners and emissaries in the fight against terrorism, fanaticism, and identity-based hatred. Only through dialogue can such assurances be mutually established.

My son Daniel was a dialogue-maker who earned respect on both sides of the East–West divide. He had an unshaken belief in the power of communication to change people's minds and hearts. In his spirit, and for the sake of my grandson's generation, we must see this dialogue continued.

Notes

1   Judea Pearl, *I am Jewish* (Woodstock, VT: Jewish Lights Publishing, 2004), p. xxv.
2   Bertrand Russell, *The Principles of Mathematics* (Cambridge: Cambridge University Press, 1903).
3   *Washington Post*, June 1, 2004, p. A23.
4   Ibid.
5   *Wall Street Journal*, May 20, 2004.
6   Shmuel Bar "The Religious Sources of Islamic Terrorism," *Policy Review* 124 (June–July 2004), pp. 27–37, p. 31.

21

The Just War Tradition and Cultural Dialogue

Jean Bethke Elshtain

At first blush it no doubt seems improbable that the just war tradition might contribute to cross-cultural dialogue. That tradition offers criteria by which to assess whether a resort to war is justified and whether the means deployed to fight a justified war are themselves just. Surely, we no doubt think, when the shooting starts, dialogue ceases; that, at least, is a common way of construing such matters. But this is a hasty judgment, or so I hope to demonstrate. In fact, the just war tradition, in rejecting any notion of total or perfect justice as the aim of war, and in recognizing that no side in a war is wholly guiltless, reminds us that we live in a world in which we are well advised to stand down from moral Manicheanism of the "we're good, they're bad" sort and to reflect critically on our own justifications and actions. This sort of reflection is the beginning of authentic cultural dialogue. By "authentic" I mean a form of dialogue that aims to clarify our differences as well as to explore our commonalities.

The full particulars of the just war tradition cannot be treated adequately in a brief essay. Suffice it to say that self-defense and protecting the innocent from certain harm – the innocent being those in no position to defend themselves – are two primary justifications for a resort to the use of force. As well, a war must be declared by a legal authority and must be pursued without vindictiveness. In the course of war-fighting, two principal norms come into play. The first, discrimination, requires that soldiers do everything possible to distinguish combatants from non-combatants as targets. The second, proportionality, demands that no force beyond what is minimally required in order to accomplish a war aim be utilized, and that force be proportional to the offense incurred. Even a person unfamiliar with the just war tradition can readily see that the overall aim of this way of thinking about war in ethical terms is to minimize both the occasions for war and war's destructiveness, once embarked upon.

But there is more that needs to be said. The just war tradition insists that a *political* ethic is an ethic of responsibility. This way of thinking rejects both the "anything goes" ethic of stern Machiavellian *realpolitik* and, as well, a stance that foreswears action if that action commits a nation to the use of armed force in a responsible, because limited, way. The just war tradition calls us to concrete responsibility for our own people and, as well, for others who may not be among our citizens but may be in need, often desperate need, of protection from those who mean to harm and destroy them. Looking back at American – and world – inaction during the horrific slaughter of Rwandan Tutsis by Rwandan Hutus in 1994, we are rightly horrified and ashamed. Surely those who might have acted to forestall this slaughter or to ameliorate it should have. The just war tradition teaches us that refusing to deploy force in the interest of justice makes decision-makers every bit as culpable as are those who deploy force badly and in the absence of appropriate restraint.

These are the basic lineaments of the tradition. How can it contribute directly to cultural dialogue? How might it help us to avoid a melodramatic "clash of civilizations"? The just war tradition helps us to appreciate that, in combat, both one's own soldiers and enemy combatants are moral equals, if you will. Each faces the other, armed, and may harm or kill the other. The rough-and-ready equality of the battlefield often has profound effects on soldiers. They find themselves incapable of thinking about an abstract, anonymous enemy. They recognize that the soldiers they face on the other side are human beings with their own hopes and dreams, human beings whose lives are precious to them and to those who love them. Soldiers understand that many enemy combatants have children and, if the soldier dies, these children will grow up without a father. (Despite the presence of women in the military of the United States, it remains the case that nearly all actual fighting takes place between units that are overwhelmingly male. All one need do is to look at casualty lists from the Iraq War and to note the gender gap in order to confirm this observation.) All of these factors compel certain forms of moral recognition that diminish rather than stoke hatred and animosity over the long run.

Forms of battlefield recognition remind us that a central feature of the just war tradition is that every nation and every people is part of a complex mosaic of cultures and traditions. Even as we are loyal to our tradition, so others are loyal to theirs. There are terrible moments when a political movement or regime is destructive of the culture of its own nation: Nazi Germany, Stalin's Soviet Union, and Saddam Hussein's Iraq come to mind. In such circumstances, we recognize that if we are fighting, we are not fighting entire cultures and peoples but, rather, those who have seized a nation and distorted its traditions in the service of their tyrannical purposes. Similarly, as President George W. Bush insisted from the first moment after the horrors of September 11, 2001, the United States is not at war against the great tradition that is Islam but, rather, is fighting those who defame that tradition in order that it might serve as a goad to, and justification for, the murder of thousands of innocents. No clash of civilizations, then, so much as a war against those who seek such a clash, desire an absolutist confrontation, and act in a manner that repudiates any limits and any other possibilities. In his multiple fatwas, Osama bin Laden has called repeatedly on all Muslims to kill all Americans whenever and wherever they may be found. This is the sort of moral fanaticism the just war tradition prohibits, by restricting both the occasions for war and the universe of who may be justly fought, and how. In a totalized war of the sort assumed by bin Laden, there is no possibility for one side to attempt to understand the other; it is either destroy utterly or be destroyed utterly.

But the just war tradition points us in a different direction. It reminds us that no nation has an exclusive purchase on political reason, justice, and decency. It reminds us that even those of good purpose may go astray and act badly. And it also reminds us that, at times, those who are fighting for an evil cause, like Nazi Germany, may nonetheless fight in honorable ways that are obedient to the laws of war, whose codification over the centuries owes so much to the just war tradition. Within just war teaching, the "other side" gains a voice and proffers reasons and its own forms of justification. (Or, at least, this possibility exists.) As well, we are obliged to assess critically our own motivations and our own deeds. In so doing, just war helps to keep alive and open the possibility for mediation, arbitration, and negotiation along the way. In resisting extremism, just war nurtures the possibility of mutual understanding and rejects the view that "we" have nothing in common with "them." It is vital to hold out the prospect of peace as a form of mutual recognition, even in a time of war.

22

Celebrating Differences on our Melting Pot Planet

Prince El Hassan bin Talal

The feeling of global insecurity has seldom, if ever, been greater than it is today.

Kofi Annan, UN Secretary-General, Message to the
37th Plenary of the Assembly of the World Federation
of UNAs, Barcelona, May 8–11, 2003

Cemal Kafadar, in his *Between Two Worlds: The Construction of the Ottoman State*,[1] argues that, "One is not necessarily born into a people; one may also become of a people, within a socially constructed dialect of inclusions and exclusions." From an Islamic theological perspective, everybody that is born to this world is born free and equal and innocent, in the fullest sense of those terms. Difference, therefore, according to the Qur'an, is not only to be tolerated and accepted, it is to be celebrated as the object of creation itself. The principal governing relation between humans is, the Qur'an tells us, *atta`aruf*, or acquaintance: *O people! We have formed you into nations and tribes so that you may know one another* (49: 13).[2]

The Qur'an is thus a pluralistic scripture,[3] affirmative of other traditions. And Islam is a pluralistic vision of civilizational solidarity, expressed through *Tawheed*, or the essential unity of creation; a space, both existential and material, in which Muslims are commanded by God to respect others. It is a civilization also

... the fullest sense of the word. Yet the assumption that Islam and democracy, or Islam and human rights, are somehow antithetical,[4] is the preferred assumption of many scholars and political leaderships today. Perhaps this is because things "Islamic" are today more often than not equated with things "illiberal." However, whereas concepts such as accountability and even democracy may be relatively new in the field of international relations[5] (as understood in the secular liberal context of modern Western civilization), in Islam these are age-old precepts, and therefore the foundation from which a dialogue of civilizations is constructed.

Appeals for an understanding and appreciation of Islam's contribution to human civilization would probably fall on many deaf ears today, notably the neo-conservatives for whom the terms of a dialogue among civilizations must necessarily be dictated by the imperative of a new "war against terrorism." US Secretary of Defense Paul Wolfowitz, in a recent speech,[6] was liberal to the hilt when he said: "We must speak to the hundreds of millions of moderate and tolerant people in the Muslim world . . . who aspire to enjoy the blessings of freedom and democracy and free enterprise," but conservative to the core when he stated that terrorists "target not only the West, but their *fellow* Muslims." Most Muslims, like most Christians, Jews, Buddhists, Hindus, Sikhs, and people of faith and no faith everywhere, would rightly take issue with such a similitude, however. As Mehri Niknam, executive director of The Maimonides Foundation, London, reminds us: "Religions cannot be isolationist, and communities need to interact." Neither, of course, can the process of Enlightenment be ignored by religions, since that encompasses the inclusive and confluent notions of civil liberty and religious freedom.[7]

Anybody who seeks an enlightened understanding of Islamic civilization's contribution to Enlightenment need only refer to Ibn Khaldun's *al-Muqaddimah* (*prolegomena*), written in 1377, in the "ignorant" Middle Ages that some would urge "moderate and tolerant" Muslims to throw into the dustbin of history. This presented a sophisticated analysis of free market economics and the rule of law, which remains the antithesis of Islamist radicalism found in parts of the Muslim world today. Indeed, even after six centuries, the thoughts of Ibn Khaldun stand up remarkably well to neo-conservative notions of an impending clash of civilizations. Ibn Khaldun's philosophy of history argues that civilization (*imran*) arises only where there is *asabiyah* – solidarity – the consciousness of communal or blood ties, which in the modern era one might reinterpret as civilizational solidarity.[8]

Perhaps this was the primary intellectual inspiration behind the diplomatic assertion of President Sayyed Muhammad Khatami (President of the Islamic Republic of Iran and President of the Islamic Conference Organization) of an Islamic initiative for a dialogue among civilizations. His stated basis for doing so was "rationality as the origin of wisdom"[9] in terms of both understanding and participating in such dialogue. This is also a radical departure from the accommodationism of détente[10] as a tool for managing international, especially superpower, relations. But if dialogue is the antidote to a clash of civilizations, détente ought now to be revisited in another, less belligerent context.

The dialogue of civilizations initiative shows that "religions are more than collections of doctrines."[11] They have important practical dimensions too. The call to Islam is certainly a call to unity of belief, but it is also a call to unity of purpose and a recognition, through civilizational solidarity, of our common humanity: "*He has laid down for you the religion which He enjoined upon Noah, and which We revealed to you, and which We enjoined upon Abraham, Moses and Jesus: Establish the religion, and be not divided therein.*"[12]

But the concept of civilizational solidarity should not be limited to an appeal for support of the popular idea of "common humanity." It should be motivated by enlightened self-interest as the driving force behind policy-making processes in meeting contemporary challenges. There is a distinction here between politics and policies, particularly in terms of the interactions between people who live cross-civilizational, cross-cultural lives. Roberto Toscano, an Italian diplomat, argues that much will depend on minority communities themselves. He focuses particularly on Muslim communities in the West[13] and their capacity to choose the right representatives, interact with authorities, and successfully combine attachment to religion and their own traditional cultures with ratic citizenship. Indeed, his premise is that the "liberal" prospect of "integration without assimilation" will reject external factors such as the threat of international terrorism. He explains that we will move toward a situation in which it will be more correct to speak of "European Muslims" just as we speak of "American Catholics." But this will not happen unless and until the "West" acknowledges its Judaeo-Christian-Islamic heritage. Islam is not a geopolitical entity, but a universal message capable of integration with diverse and very different cultures, including American and European.

Ethics is central to an understanding of common humanity and to finding an answer to the world *problématique*. There is an urgent need to develop, globally, a universally acceptable ethic of human solidarity, on a par with civilizational solidarity. In encompassing the ethics of human solidarity, we encompass the forces of change, the young, the uprooted, the neglected, man-made disasters, and industrial disasters. This allows us also to admit that problems cannot be dealt with in isolation; nor can they be evaluated only by considering short-term benefits and ignoring long-term effects. Our very existence depends on the actions and lives of other people. Interdependence requires that *all* economies depend upon international stability and on a rule-based system of global governance. Interdependence is both a prerequisite for, and consequence of, a dialogue among civilizations.

Also implicit in this ethic of human solidarity is the requirement for an overarching matrix of International Humanitarian and Human Rights Law. Every topic one could think of in terms of the conflict between man and man, between man and nature, between natural disasters and man-made disasters, falls somewhere within this matrix. Yet, sadly, despite all our technical, financial, and human resources, the world has continued to become richer in problems and poorer in solutions.

How can ethical change be brought about within an exclusionist discourse? I believe that some of the basic concepts need to be revisited through a dialogue of civilizations. Poverty and inequality are our enemies, and indeed, "to fight poverty is to fight the war to end all wars, and to win that war is the only way to go beyond winning wars in the traditional sense of winning lasting peace."[14] But can we not redefine poverty in terms of human well-being rather than in terms of dollars and cents? Poverty, which according to Imam Ali bin Abi Talib, "undermines religion, subverts reason and invites hatred," can be tackled as a root cause only if we humanize economics and politics, putting human well-being at the center of national, as well as global, policymaking. Perhaps the time has come to promote a culture of peace as opposed to the mere absence of war.

In the new millennium, issues of responsibility have assumed a new dimension. Humankind, still beset by conflict and violence, faces new global challenges. It is in this context that the Parliament of Cultures was born as an intra-regional attempt at establishing the parameters for conversation and dialogue among participants in the region; a platform for encouraging inter-regional conversations between a particular region and other regions of the world; and the foundation for building a practical bridge between cultures, not least locating and emphasizing those things – values, purpose, and vision – that all civilizations share and will continue to share regardless of differences.

The specter of a clash of civilizations ought to be erased from our minds. As a Muslim, I believe that Islam teaches a transcendent morality, championing pluralism and condemning all forms of intolerance.[15] Taken to its logical conclusion, the clash of civilizations idea is both a politically fundamentalist and psychologically separatist theory that might be more aptly described as neo-conservative fundamentalism.

It is only through thinking globally and acting regionally that we can enhance that which is universal while respecting differences. Whether or not history has come to an end, or whether or not we are heading for a clash of civilizations, is not really the point. What is needed is to create programs and ideas that bring certain unacceptables to an end: war, terror, violence, and disregard for the inherent dignity of humanity.

In the age of a fear of dominance by a single melting pot "civilization," it is only right that common humanity acknowledges the contributions of *all* civilizations and living cultures to our melting pot planet.

Notes

1 Cemal Kafadar, *Between Two Worlds: The Construction of the Ottoman State* (Berkeley: University of California Press, 2002).
2 *The Holy Qur'an*, 4th US edn, trans. M. H. Shakir (Elmhurst, NY: Tahrike Tarsile Qur'an, Inc. 1991).
3 David Zeidan, "The Islamist Fundamentalist View of Life as a Perennial Battle," *MERIA Journal*, 5 (Dec. 2001).
4 Katerina Dalacoura, *Islam, Liberalism and Human Rights* (London: I. B. Tauris & Co. Ltd, 2003; New York: Palgrave Macmillan, 2003).
5 Jacques Forster (vice-president, ICRC), "War and Accountability," *FORUM* (April 2002).
6 Paul Wolfowitz, "Bridging the Gap with the Muslim World," Asia Security Conference: The Shangri-La Dialogue, Singapore, June 1, 2002.
7 Mehri Niknam, "The Lessons of September 11: A Judaeo-Islamic Interfaith Perspective," Speech presented to the International Symposium on Islamic Responses to Terrorism, Al-Khoei Foundation, London, November 2001.
8 Benjamin Schwarz and Christopher Layne, "The Hard Questions, A New Grand Strategy," *The Atlantic Monthly*, 289 (January 2002), pp. 36–42.
9 Sayyed Muhammad Khatami, Address to the European University Institute, Florence, Italy, March 10, 1999.
10 Schwarz and Layne, "Hard Questions."
11 Muhammad Legenhausen, "Islam and Religious Pluralism," *al-Tawhid*, 14/3 (Winter 1998), Qom, Iran.
12 *The Holy Qur'an*, 42.13.
13 Roberto Toscano, *Assimilation without Integration: An Italian Perspective*, ed. Sayyed Nadeem Kazmi (London: Dialogue, 2001).
14 Eveline Herfkens, UN Secretary-General's Executive Coordinator for the Millennium Development Goals Campaign, Statement to WFUNA, May 9, 2003.
15 Ahmed H. Al-Rahim, "A New Agenda for American Muslims," *Boston Globe*, January 16, 2002.

Part IV
From Concern to Action

23

Clash or Dialogue of Cultures?

Bernard Lewis

In a sense, the dialogue between cultures has been going on since the beginning of recorded history, as different cultures arose, expanded, and in time met. True, the meeting was often hostile, more a clash than a dialogue, but this was not always so, and even cultures at war continued to exchange commodities and skills, knowledge and ideas, to their mutual advantage.

The best-known and most enduring of such encounters took place between Islam and Christendom. At first, the picture does not look promising – the recurring pattern of holy wars both ways, of conquest and reconquest, of attack and counterattack. This was the longest struggle known to history, and for some it is still going on.

But not for all, and for those who seek dialogue rather than confrontation there is much that is encouraging. True, there has been a long and intense struggle, but the two sides were thrown together less by their differences – though these are not insignificant – than by their resemblances, which are profound and pervasive. Both share a common heritage from the past, from the ancient civilizations of the eastern Mediterranean and the Middle East; both share certain basic beliefs about the nature of the universe; both in the past have shared – and many still share – the same sense of mission to bring these truths to all mankind.

In these resemblances, even in the nature and purpose of past conflict, we may find hope of dialogue. Today, there are elements on both sides that seek such dialogue; others that prepare for a final clash. Each side will have to make its own choice.

24

The Fellowship of Dialogue

James D. Wolfensohn

One of the most enticing political theories advanced in the aftermath of the cold war was that of a "clash of civilizations"[1]. According to this projection, longstanding ideological fault lines would soon give way to a new global tectonics in which conflicts emerged, not from economic or political roots, but from cultural ones. After the 2001 terrorist attack on the World Trade Center, this theory resonated once again, raising fears of a confrontation between Islam and the West.

I do not subscribe to the inevitability of culture clash or a world divided. To be sure, my generation grew up thinking that there were two worlds, the haves and the have-nots, and that they were, for the most part, quite separate. But that was wrong then, and it is even more wrong now. The wall that many people imagined to separate the rich countries from the poor countries fell along with the twin towers on September 11.

In his famous passage about "seeing through a glass darkly," St Paul wrote: "When I was a child, I spake as a child, I understood as a child, I thought as a child: but when I became a man, I put away childish things." We know better now, that ours is one world, not two, and we must look with a clear eye to the future.

Six billion people inhabit the world today, all but 1 billion in developing countries. Close to 2 billion more people will soon join our planet, with, again, all but 50 million born in the developing world. Today, half of the world's population is under the age of 25. Many are experiencing poverty and unemployment, and many are disillusioned by what they see as an inequitable global system. A growing number are leaving their home countries to find work. Migration is a critical issue, and remittances – money sent home by foreign workers – now exceed official development assistance.

We are linked in so many ways: not only by trade, finance, and migration, but also by environment, disease, drugs, crime, conflict, and, yes, terrorism. We are linked, rich and poor alike, by a shared desire to leave a better world to our children. And by the realization that if we fail in one part of the planet, the rest becomes vulnerable. This is the true meaning of globalization.

Learning about other countries and cultures and respecting their values and aspirations is imperative. Growing up in Australia, I learned a great deal about the monarchs of Europe and very little about the rich history of my Asian neighbors. People young and old today need to know about Islam, India, China, and Africa. We must prepare ourselves for life in a different, more diverse, and culturally abundant world.

Communities of faith have a particular role to play here in putting our one world in perspective, forging unity within diversity, and in encouraging the fellowship of dialogue.

From Dialogue to Action

In the fall of 2003, I met in Paris with youth leaders who represented organizations with more than 120 million members worldwide. I met with a still broader group in Sarajevo in September 2004. These gatherings included rural youth and street children orphaned by AIDS and civil conflict, youth from the excluded Roma community, and young people with disabilities. As it happened, they also reflected a wide range of religious backgrounds.

They met in peace and with mutual respect. They wondered why my generation finds it so difficult to do the same. They said they are ready to be part of the solution, to be partners. But they also said that they do not want a future based only on economic considerations; there must be something more. They challenged us about values and beliefs.

We must, together with them, take up that challenge.

The Prophet Muhammad wrote: "God changes not what is in a people, until they change what is in themselves."

We cannot stand idly by while over a billion people struggle to survive on less than a dollar a day, as 3 million people die annually from HIV/AIDS, with over 2 million of those deaths in sub-Saharan Africa, when over 100 million children never see the inside of a school, when there are no jobs for hundreds of millions of young people across many regions. All cultures, all religions, stand for hope. For people without hope, violence is too often a last refuge.

In recent months, Iraq, Afghanistan, and the Middle East have dominated the headlines. But in the last dozen years, there were 56 major armed conflicts in 44 different places. Eighty percent of the world's 20 poorest countries have suffered a major civil war over this period. Since 1998 some 3 million people have died in conflict in Congo alone.

We must redress the imbalances, in terms of resources and rights, between rich and poor. Poverty and insecurity anywhere have repercussions, often direct and immediate, on other, distant parts of the globe. Global poverty and security are intimately linked, as never before.

We must fulfill the promises world leaders made in the Millennium Development Goals and at the subsequent summit meetings in Monterrey and Johannesburg, scaling up our efforts to deliver on economic growth and opportunity, on education and health care, on clean air and water, and on equity and social justice. The work falls to both developed and developing country leaders to make the case – and create the environment – for poverty reduction and peace.

We know elections are won and lost on local issues. Pensions, health care, and jobs are the hot topics in political debates, with hardly a word said about development. But it is global issues, and especially poverty, that will shape the world in which our children will live. Development and the fight against poverty are domestic issues as well as international issues.

At present, the international community's commitment to address these imbalances falls woefully short of what is required. Aid today is close to its lowest level ever. It has fallen by half, from 0.5 percent of Gross Domestic Product in the early 1960s to 0.25 percent today. And this at a time when incomes in developed countries have never been higher.

While rich countries spend about $700 billion on military defense and $300 billion to subsidize food, they spend just $68 billion on official development assistance. These numbers speak volumes. They are a call to fellowship, to dialogue, to change.

Different Religions, Common Purpose

The interconnections and the interdependence of this world are real, longstanding, and advancing at a rapid rate, expressing themselves in a myriad of ways. Far from suggesting that one culture or religion must be subsumed by another, the question and the challenge for us all are how to foster tolerance, understanding, and respect among different countries, different cultures, and different religions.

This requires a new inclusiveness, bringing culture and religion into the recognized legitimate discourse of international statecraft and development. Culture and faith are not theoretical issues but very practical ones. Without a better understanding of the underlying forces of history, religion, and culture, any efforts to bring about peace, development, poverty alleviation, and higher standards for governance and economic planning will be frustrated. There is a need to reach out to leaders of different cultures and religions to better understand these issues and how to integrate them into programs to reestablish security and promote sustainable economic development.

In particular, we have much to learn from moderate Muslim communities, whose spokespersons and leaders should be recognized as real sources of knowledge and potential solutions, and not just cultivated as allies of convenience.

As many readers will recognize, partnership and dialogue among the faiths and the development community are a special concern of mine, one that has engendered considerable debate and discussion within the World Bank. Faith-based organizations have reach and influence, in developed and developing countries, on a wide array of issues, spiritual and practical. Faith organizations are uniquely well positioned to advocate on behalf of the poor for increasing social justice and redressing global imbalances.

Especially in developing countries, faith-based organizations are well grounded in local culture and understand the roots and coping mechanisms of poverty. They interact with the community on practical matters that concern their daily lives – at birth, death, and marriage, in time of crisis – hence they are uniquely positioned to influence values and behaviors. No other institutions have comparable access to communities and households through such well-developed networks on the ground.

Documentation of grassroots testimony and perception, including the study, *Voices of the Poor*,[2] published by the World Bank, show that faith institutions, especially at the local level, inspire greater levels of trust and confidence than governments, donors, or secular non-governmental groups. Moreover, faith-based organizations are hugely important providers of social services. In many countries, they are the source of half or more of health and education services. In countries and areas in conflict, they are often the only source of social services. This is a constituency that has earned its place at the table.

Harmony among religions, celebrating differences, is possible. I have seen it – for example, in African communities where people show respect for others' beliefs and religions, without attempting to tamper with long-cherished credos.

It should never be conceded that the goal of religious harmony is unattainable. It is certainly a possibility, provided it is seen as a practical, humanitarian strategy and not as a pretext for making ideological changes. Most holy scriptures contain words to this effect. The Qur'an, for instance, says:

> Surely those who believe, those who are Jewish, the Christians, and the converts; anyone who (1) believes in God, and (2) believes in the Last Day, and (3) leads a righteous life, will receive their recompense from their Lord. They have nothing to fear, nor will they grieve. (2: 62)

In a similar vein, Pope John Paul has stated: "To do harm or promote violence and conflict in the name of religion is a terrible contradiction and a great offense against God." To use religion to fan unrest and cloak violence contradicts the teachings of all the world's great religions. Terrorists should be called to task for what they are: enemies of peace and tolerance and roadblocks to conquering global poverty.

One Family: Humanity

Bringing our one world into balance demands the participation of all sectors of society as one family. Taking successful projects and scaling them up to benefit millions of people, not just thousands, requires strong partnerships among governments, business, civil society, and the multilateral and bilateral institutions.

Non-governmental organizations have increased in size, scale, knowledge, and experience. They are now fundamental to development across a broad range of activities. Likewise, the private sector is an increasingly important voice, not only in generating growth and opportunity, but also in terms of corporate social responsibility, environmental conservation, and the delivery of social services.

Better living standards, better education and access to health care, and equity are the foundation for hope, not only for poor people, but for all the world's people. The dream of the World Bank is a world free of poverty. This is not just a moral or ethical issue. It is the basis for global security. The primary issue, then, is how committed and serious the world is about reaching this objective and providing the resources needed to make it a reality.

We must be forthright in our dialogue and resolute in action, drawing on shared values and beliefs to fulfill the promise of our age. As the Psalmist of the Old Testament said, we can be like "the tree planted by the rivers of water, that bringeth forth his fruit in his season; his leaf also shall not wither; and whatsoever he doeth shall prosper" (Psalm 1: 3).

Notes

1 Samuel P. Huntington, "Clash of Civilizations?," *Foreign Affairs*, 72 (Summer 1993): 22–49, and *idem, The Clash of Civilizations and the Remaking of the World Order* (New York: Simon and Schuster, 1996).
2 Deepa Narayan et al., *Voices of the Poor: Can Anyone Hear Us?* (Washington, DC: World Bank, 2000).

25

Hard Power and Soft Power

Joseph S. Nye Jr

International politics has long been described in terms of states seeking power and security in an anarchic world. States form alliances and balance the power of others in order to preserve their independence. Traditionally, we spoke of states as unitary rational actors. "France allied with Britain because it feared Germany." There was little room for morality or idealism – or for actors other than states.

Transnational relations, however, can no longer be ignored. On September 11, 2001, a transnational terrorist organization killed more Americans than did the nation of Japan on December 7, 1941. The national security strategy of the United States now states that "we are menaced less by fleets and armies than by catastrophic technologies falling into the hands of the embittered few." Instead of strategic rivalry, "today the world's great powers find ourselves on the same side – united by common dangers of terrorist violence and chaos."

Military power and economic power are both examples of "hard" command power that can be used to get others to change their position. Hard power can rest on inducements ("carrots") or threats ("sticks"). But there is also an indirect way to get the outcomes that you want that could be called "the second face of power." A country may obtain its preferred outcomes in world politics because other countries want to follow it, admiring its values, emulating its example, aspiring to its level of prosperity and openness. In this sense, it is just as important to set the agenda and attract others in world politics as it is to force them to change through the threat or use of military or economic weapons. This soft power – getting others to want the outcomes that you want – co-opts people rather than coerces them.

Think of the impact of young people behind the Iron Curtain listening to American music and news on Radio Free Europe; of Chinese students symbolizing their protests in Tiananmen Square by creating a replica of the Statue of Liberty. When you can get others to want what you want, you do not have to spend as much on sticks and carrots to move them in your direction.

The ability to establish preferences tends to be associated with intangible power resources such as an attractive culture, political values and institutions, and policies that are seen as legitimate or having moral authority. If I can get you to want to do what I want, then I do not have to force you to do what you do not want. If a country represents values that others want to follow, it will cost less to lead. Soft power is far more than the influence of Coca-Cola and blue jeans, though this distinction is lost on some skeptics. The ability of a country to attract others arises from its culture, its values and domestic practices, and the perceived legitimacy of its foreign policies. When our policies are seen as legitimate in the eyes of others, our soft power is enhanced.

While the United States enjoys unprecedented military power, it is not nearly as dominant on economic issues (where Europe acts collectively). The information revolution and globalization empower non-state actors on transnational issues in ways far greater than anything encountered in the 1970s. The result is a complex, three-dimensional set of issues in world politics, each possessing a different structure in the distribution of power. While the distribution of power on military issues is unipolar, it makes no sense to use traditional terms like unipolarity and hegemony to describe the distribution of power on economic and transnational issues, where the United States needs the help of others to obtain its preferred outcomes. Hard power remains crucial in a world of states trying to guard their independence and terrorist organizations willing to turn to violence. But soft power will become increasingly important in preventing terrorists from recruiting supporters, and for dealing with transnational issues that require multilateral cooperation.

Much of this became blindingly obvious after September 11, 2001, when a global network of non-state actors attacked the United States. Globalization is more than just an economic phenomenon, and it had been shrinking the natural buffers that distance and two oceans traditionally provided. September 11 also dramatized how the information revolution and technological change have elevated the importance of transnational issues and empowered non-state actors to play a larger role in world politics. A few decades ago, instantaneous global communications were out of the financial reach of all but governments or large organizations like transnational corporations or the Catholic Church. At the same time, the US and the USSR were secretly spending billions of dollars on overhead space photography. Now commercial one-meter resolution photos are cheaply available to anyone, and the internet enabled 1,500 NGOs to inexpensively coordinate the "battle of Seattle" that disrupted meetings of the World Trade Organization.

Most worrying are the effects of these deep trends on terrorism. Terrorism is nothing new, but the "democratization of technology" has increased the lethality and agility of terrorists over the past decades, and the trend is likely to continue. In the twentieth century, a pathological individual like Hitler or Stalin needed the power of a government to be able to kill millions of people. If twenty-first-century terrorists get hold of weapons of mass destruction, that power of destruction will for the first time be available to deviant groups and individuals. Traditional state-centric analysts think that punishing states that sponsor terrorism can solve the problem. It can help, but it does not remove the effects of the democratization of technology empowering individuals. This "privatization of war" is not only a major historical change in world politics; the potential impact if terrorists obtained nuclear weapons could drastically alter the nature of modern cities and contemporary civilization.

In the current "war on terrorism," the American military easily toppled the Taliban government in Afghanistan, but it appears to have destroyed only a quarter to a third of the Al Qaeda network with its cells in more than 50 countries. Unilateral military solutions would be out of the question because of cells in friendly countries. Success at stemming terrorism requires years of patient civilian cooperation with others in intelligence sharing, police work, and tracing of financial flows. Such a war cannot be won unilaterally with orders from imperial headquarters.

Dealing with the new challenges will depend not just on military and economic might, but on the soft power of culture and values, and on pursuing policies that make others feel that they have been consulted and their interests taken into account. As the German editor Josef Joffe has said, "unlike centuries past, when war was the great arbiter, today the most interesting types of power do not come out of the barrel of a gun. . . .Today there is a much bigger payoff in "getting others to want what you want," and that has to do with cultural attraction and ideology and agenda setting and holding out big prizes for cooperation."[1]

A critical step in tackling the challenges facing us today will be the development of a long-term strategy of cultural and educational exchanges that develop a richer and more open civil society in Middle Eastern countries. Much of this work can be promoted by corporations, foundations, universities, and other non-profit organizations, as well as by governments. There are many strands to a strategy for creating soft-power resources and promoting conditions for the development of democracy. But none will be effective unless the style and substance of American policies are consistent with the larger democratic message.

Because the war on terrorism involves a civil war between radicals and moderates within Islamic civilization, the soft power of the Islamists is a disturbing symptom and a warning of the need for Americans and others to find better ways of projecting soft power to strengthen the moderates. Moderate churches and synagogues can play a role with moderate Muslims. In all three religions the prophet Abraham is a revered figure, so the idea of an Abrahamic dialogue among Muslims, Christians, and Jews may be an example of the ways that non-governmental actors can exercise their soft power and create bridges of understanding.

Above all, Americans will have to become more aware of cultural differences. We must become less parochial, and more sensitive to foreign perceptions. The first step in making a better case is a greater understanding of how our policies appear to others and of the cultural filters that affect how they hear our messages. Using soft power more effectively will require changing attitudes at home as well as abroad. To put it bluntly, Americans need to listen. Wielding soft power is far less unilateral than employing hard power, and we need to learn that lesson if we are to succeed in winning the cooperation of others who share our fundamental goals of making the world freer and more secure.

Note

1 Josef Joffe, "America the Inescapable," *New York Times Magazine*, June 8, 1997, p. 38.

26

Global Governance in an Interdependent World

Benjamin R. Barber

The war in Iraq with its terrorist horrors and unsettling American prison abuses, along with the unraveling of the American effort at democratization, has captured the world's attention. But lurking in the background is the issue of global governance, which remains the world's most pressing business and its most daunting challenge. Despite almost 60 years of productive common experience, not even Europe has achieved common democratic governance. The seams in its tacked-together common union are showing – the Swedish no vote on the euro, the continuing Danish and English skepticism, the complications engendered by the effort to extend the market to Turkey and to absorb the 15 new nations now formally part of what was once a six-country mini-federation. The United Nations, the great hope of the post-Second World War world, remains an unwieldy conglomerate of quarreling factions and adversarial blocs in which both the First and the Third World feel underrepresented and which often seems incapable of responding to crises and hence facilitates rather than impedes big power grandstanding. And the United States, the architect of the new international system that came out of the Second World War, appears to have turned its back on its own creation and preferred to depend on unilateralism and war rather than multilateralism and law in pursuit of security – its misadventures in Iraq being but the leading edge of this tendency. In short, as the need for regional and global governance has grown, the likelihood of actually achieving it seems to have diminished.

And yet, and yet! The devastating events of September 11, 2001, that made evident how far the world is from a common peace, also spoke with a vengeance to the reality of a growing global interdependence that makes global governance ever more necessary and, probably, inevitable. For the real lesson of 9/11 points to a common world's ever more common destiny.

Europe has already learned the lesson of interdependence from the Second World War, if not before, while the Third World, deeply dependent on what happens in the First World, has never harbored any illusions of real independence. But the United States, the key to global governance today, has been and remains the world's leading promoter of the idea of independence.

After all, 228 years ago, in the belief that liberty and the autonomy of the sovereign nation went hand in hand, America proclaimed its independence. For more than two centuries it has pursued the sovereign ideal as the premise of the rights and social justice in whose name it has striven to become both democratic and free. Speaking not just for itself but for other nations, it has (as President Bush did in 2003 at the United Nations) insisted that democracy is premised on national liberation, and that personal liberty requires national independence.

A little less than 15 years ago, people in Budapest, Prague, Warsaw, Moscow, and elsewhere throughout Eastern Europe and Asia reasserted the powerful connection between liberty and independence by declaring their own liberation from the dominion of Soviet communism – reclaiming their liberty by reasserting their right to be self-governing. Yet, though today these same nations are pressing to join Europe, in other parts of the world as different as Afghanistan, Liberia, Kosovo, and Brazil, nations continue to reassert their sovereign independence from domestic tyranny and foreign imperialism as the condition for the liberty of their people.

With recent history as their tutor, however, nations that have long cherished their independence or recently struggled to achieve it are learning the hard way that there is neither freedom nor equality nor safety from tyranny nor security from terror on the basis of independence alone. That in a world in which ecology, public health, markets, technology, and war affect everyone equally, interdependence is a stark reality upon which the survival of the human race depends. That where fear rules, and terrorism is met by "shock and awe" only, neither peace nor democracy can ensue. That while we have yet to construct those global institutions that might offer us a benevolent interdependence, we are beset by global entities that impose on us the costs of a malevolent and often anarchic interdependence. That in the absence of a new journey to democratize our interdependence, we may lose the blessings conferred by the old journey to democratic independence.

Where once nations depended on sovereignty alone to secure their destinies, today they depend on one other. In a world where the poverty of some imperils the wealth of others, where none are safer than the least safe, multilateralism is not a stratagem of idealists but a realist necessity. The lesson of 9/11 was not that rogue states could be unilaterally preempted and vanquished by a sovereign United States, but that sovereignty was a chimera. HIV and global warming and international trade and nuclear proliferation and transnational crime and predatory capital had already stolen from America the substance of its cherished sovereignty well before the terrorists displayed their murderous contempt for it on that fateful morning.

The irony is, then, that while sovereignty remains the first principle of international affairs for the United States, its reality has already been fatally compromised by the realities of interdependence. Even as the United States refuses to place its troops under foreign commanders and promulgates a preventive war doctrine that gives it the sovereign right to decide when and where and against whom it will wage war, it suffers from an ever weakening sovereignty in other key areas. Despite its global economic hegemony, Washington can no longer prevent a single job or factory or company from leaving the United States for more profitable venues elsewhere, cannot stop alien viruses from entering its territory, cannot control financial capital, cannot prevent intellectual piracy on the internet. Sovereignty remains a powerful word and the justification for a great deal of what nations do today, but as a reality it has lost much of its potency. Terrorism, like all international crime, testifies to the insufficiencies of sovereignty. The United States could protect neither the capital of finance at the World Trade Center nor the headquarters of its vaunted military machine at the Pentagon, despite the fact that the "invading force" was armed only with box-cutters and fanatic zeal. Indeed, the hijackers came from inside the US, not outside, and the "states that harbored them" prior to the attack were not Afghanistan and Iraq but New Jersey and Florida. So much for sovereignty!

Yet America still seems to prefer to play the lone ranger – Gary Cooper in the film *High Noon*, where the sheriff must take on four desperadoes all by himself.

Recent events suggest, however, that this is a world where only global posses – communities working together – have a chance of succeeding. Interdependence is now our reality, and the acknowledgment of interdependence the necessary starting point for prudent foreign policy. After all, terrorists are not nations, and whether or not they are supported by rogue states, they are in effect malevolent NGOs that operate in the interstices of the international system. They use the new transnational networks of finance, telecommunications, transportation, and trade to do their business across national borders. If the states that confront them cannot use international tools at least as effectively as the terrorists use them, there is little hope that terrorism can be overcome.

Yet, while international cooperation is desirable and necessary, it is clear that the obstacles that still stand before those who seek new institutions of global governance are as various as they are intractable. The refusal of the United States under the Bush administration to negotiate an understanding that might allow it to sign the Landmines Treaty (already signed by over 140 nations) is an example. The United States has good reason to expect the Treaty signatories to recognize its special responsibilities as a global policeman and the role mines can play in protecting thinly deployed troops. But by the same token the United States has an obligation to work hard to draft a treaty it is able to sign.

Some of the same problems face the new International Criminal Tribunal. The United States believes with some justification that this new court could end up as a kangaroo court for troops it deploys on behalf of UN or other peacekeeping missions. But the imperatives of interdependence call for negotiations that allow the United States to join under reasonable conditions rather than obstinate American multilateralism or obstinate international high-mindedness that chooses hypocritically to overlook the United States' special responsibilities.

In other words, whether it is the Landmines Treaty or the Criminal Court or other obligations such as the Kyoto Treaty on Global Warming or the Anti-Ballistic Missile Treaty, the current atmosphere makes the United States a stubborn loner and its international interlocutors ineffective suitors for American cooperation. The battle in the United Nations prior to the war in Iraq was typical of an America too anxious to act without multilateral cooperation and a United Nations afraid to act at all. This is in part because sovereignty remains the first principle of the United Nations. It is a congress of nations and, the Secretary-General's Office notwithstanding, represents those nations rather than the people of the world. It is not a "we the people" organization but a "we the nations that represent peoples" organization.

To be sure, the United States has been quick to play the sovereignty card, but so have the other nations of the UN when their vital interests are at stake or where they believe that their interests are better advanced outside than inside the General Assembly. Nor is America's recent critic "old Europe" (in Secretary of Defense Rumsfeld's dismissive phrase) itself free of blame for obstructing international cooperation. Its hypocritical support of agricultural and cultural subsidies for its own afflicted economic sectors despite its putative adherence to free trade doctrines even as it pressures the Third World nations to drop their own trade restrictions is evidence of this hypocrisy, which destroyed the trade talks at Cancun in the fall of 2003.

Citizens need not await presidents or governments to embrace interdependence and work to construct a civic architecture of global cooperation, however. Indeed, they cannot wait. For the challenge is how to get "sovereign" political policy to catch up to global realities. The lessons of the above tutorial suggest that global governance must be built bottom up, not top down. That it is more likely to come from transnational civic cooperation and the work of NGOs and economic organizations than from states. This is in any case how democracy is ideally constructed: create a foundation in education, free institutions, and citizenship and build a political edifice on top of that foundation once it is settled. In other words, the continuing reluctance of governments to commit in practice to the global governance ideals to which they are committed in theory need not prevent citizens from working towards greater international cooperation.

Global governance will depend in the first instance on global citizenship, which in turn will have to rest on the fashioning of a global civil society and global civic education. Citizens, whether local or global, are made, not born, educated and socialized into their roles rather than natural inhabitants of those roles. That was the lesson taught by the American founders when Thomas Jefferson and John Adams both recognized that without educated citizens the experimental new constitution would never work. In James Madison's words, a bill of rights and a constitution were not worth the parchment on which they were written in the absence of educated citizens who could make those documents work in practice.

The challenge today, then, is to create the foundations for global governance before trying to transform the UN and Bretton Woods systems into institutional global government. The tools here will be technologies like the internet (already being used by malevolent NGOs such as Al Qaeda and international right-wing movements like the Nazis) and cooperation among NGOs on the model of the Community of Democracy and Jubilee 2000 (aiming to erase Third World debt). Their spirit has been expressed in the new Declaration of Interdependence, promulgated in 2003 and celebrated in a first "Interdependence Day" festival in Philadelphia and Budapest in 2003 and again in 2004 in Rome.

The Declaration of Interdependence captures the spirit of civic globalism:

Declaration of Interdependence

We the people of the world do herewith declare our interdependence both as individuals and legal persons and as peoples –

members of distinct communities and nations. We do pledge ourselves citizens of one CivWorld, civic, civil and civilized. Without prejudice to the goods and interests of our national and regional identities, we recognize our responsibilities to the common goods and liberties of humankind as a whole.

We do therefore pledge to work both directly and through the nations and communities of which we are also citizens:

> To establish democratic forms of global civil and legal governance through which our common rights can be secured and our common ends realized;

> To guarantee justice and equality for all by establishing on a firm basis the human rights of every person on the planet, ensuring that the least among us may enjoy the same liberties as the prominent and the powerful;

> To forge a safe and sustainable global environment for all – which is the condition of human survival – at a cost to peoples based on their current share in the world's wealth;

> To offer children, our common human future, special attention and protection in distributing our common goods, above all those upon which health and education depend; and

> To foster democratic policies and institutions expressing and protecting our human commonality; and still at the same time,

> To nurture free spaces in which our distinctive religious, ethnic and cultural identities may flourish and our equally worthy lives may be lived in dignity, protected from political, economic and cultural hegemony of every kind.

Interdependence Day and the Declaration of Interdependence, whose promulgation it marks, allow new global citizens to affirm the creative potential of what is for now merely a grim reality. No American child will ever again sleep safe in her bed if children in Baghdad or Karachi or Nairobi are not secure in theirs. Europeans will not be permitted to feel proud of liberty if people elsewhere feel humiliated by servitude. This is not because America is responsible for everything that has happened to others or because Europe was once the imperial colonizer of the world, but because in a world of interdependence the consequences of misery and injustice for some will be suffered by all.

Global governance is much more than a utopian dream. It is a necessity of interdependence to which there is no realistic alternative. But for it to emerge, there must first be global civil society and a global citizenry. To create them – citizen by citizen and group by group, from the bottom up – remains the challenge.

27

Getting to Peace: Awakening the Third Side

William L. Ury

No more daunting challenge faces us as human beings than learning to live together. How can we deal with our differences without either suppressing them or going to war over them? How can we create a "co-culture" of coexistence and conflict resolution – in our communities, our nations, and our world?

The Challenge

We are living in an extraordinary age when, for the first time since the origin of our species, all of humanity's tribes, more than 15,000 different ethnic groups, are in touch with one another. Future generations may call this "the age of the human family reunion."

Family reunions are often not entirely peaceful, and this one is no exception. Coming together can produce more heat than light, more conflict than understanding. "Reunion" means, in the short run at least, a heightening of hostilities as people are forced to confront their differences, as jealousies and resentments over inequities flare up, and as identities are threatened by different customs and beliefs. Never before in human evolution have people faced the challenge of living in a single community with billions of other human beings.

What future historians may find astonishing is not that there was so much conflict, but that there was not more. Even with all their disputes and occasional wars, the great majority of nations and ethnic groups coexist with one another. War is not the norm but the exception. Coexistence is not some distant ideal; it is a reality that characterizes the relationships among most nations and ethnic groups most of the time. This is not to belittle the significance of violence and war; far from it. It is just to remind us of the prosaic preponderance of peace.

The challenge humanity faces, then, is not to change one absolute, war, into another absolute, peace. It is not to go from 0 percent coexistence to 100 percent, but rather to proceed from, say, 90 percent to 99 percent.

The Potential for Transforming Conflict

Conflict is natural and even necessary to confront injustice in the world. The world may need more conflict, not less. The goal should not be to end conflict but to transform it, to change its form from violence and warfare to dialogue, negotiation, and democracy.

Conflict is like fire: natural, valuable, and potentially very dangerous. Before the twentieth century, fire was one of city dwellers' greatest fears. In a few minutes, a fire raging out of control could destroy entire neighborhoods and even cities. Yet, for all its evident danger, fire was long regarded as a natural and inevitable tragedy, part of human fate, just as violence and war are today. At some point, that perception of fire changed. In today's cities, thanks to building regulations and fireproof materials, emergency exits and smoke detectors, and fire fighters and trucks – in short, a comprehensive fire prevention system – urban dwellers live largely free of fear of devastating citywide fires.

Humanity has an analogous opportunity today when it comes to preventing destructive conflict. We can give up our belief in its inevitability and learn step by step how to prevent, resolve, and contain it. Working together, we can create a comprehensive conflict transformation system. As with fire, it is far from impossible.

I was once invited to conduct a discussion on preventing war among a group of 40 parliamentarians from 20 countries gathered at the United Nations. Since the gap was so large between the ideal of global security and the reality, I looked for a way to go beyond the usual cautious political speeches with their modest proposals and their calls to try harder. So I started the discussion with an imaginary newscast.

In the midst of a war between India and Pakistan, a reporter announced, a nuclear bomb had been dropped on an Indian city. On television and radio, people around the world almost instantly learned about the devastation and started immediately clamoring for an end not just to the Indo-Pakistani war, but to nuclear weapons and to war itself. The political shock waves were intense. I asked the 40 parliamentarians to imagine that they, as the leaders of their respective countries, were now meeting at the United Nations to decide what to do. A press conference had been scheduled two hours from then, so all eyes would be on them. Their task was to prepare a plan to reassure a panicking world.

Within two hours, 40 parliamentarians from six continents devised a basic plan for global security and, to everyone's surprise, reached unanimous agreement. I was amazed by how excited normally stolid politicians became when able to free their imaginations. I was also struck by the similarity of each individual's vision of security – from the German's to the Gambian's and from the Mexican's to the American's. Perhaps I should not have been surprised. Devising a plan for global security is not rocket science. Each parliamentarian knew from the experience of his or her own country what security required: a police force able to stop and deter violence, the control and elimination of the most destructive weapons, a democratically elected legislative body able to resolve differences peacefully, a strong court able to bring justice, and a new institution, a mediation service that would proactively seek to resolve conflicts before they escalated.

The world remains a long way from implementation of the parliamentarians' vision, but the direction is clear. None of the institutions they proposed could do the job alone, but all of them together, supplemented by strong preventive measures and supported by the world community, might just suffice.

The Third Side

At the heart of any effort to transform conflict lies the Third Side. Conflict is conventionally thought of as two-sided, one ethnic group or nation versus another. We tend to forget what the simplest societies on earth have long known, that every conflict is actually three-sided. No dispute takes place in a vacuum. Others are always around: relatives, neighbors, allies, neutrals, friends, or onlookers. Every conflict occurs within a community that constitutes the "Third Side" of any dispute.

The Third Side is the surrounding community, which serves as a *container for contention*. In the absence of that container, serious conflict between two parties all too easily turns into destructive strife. Within the container, however, conflict can be gradually transformed from confrontation to cooperation.

The Third Side is not a theoretical formula. It is a practical description of how destructive, seemingly intractable conflicts are gradually transformed, whether in South Africa, Northern Ireland, Sri Lanka, or Guatemala. Over the last 25 years serving as a mediator in a variety of the world's hot spots, I have witnessed the Third Side at work bringing about progress towards peace that few expected.

The Third Side is composed of outsiders, but more importantly of insiders, people with close ties to one side or the other who speak up against violence and for dialogue and negotiation. The outsiders work to support the insiders. In the case of South Africa, for example, the outside world opposed the institutionalized racism of the apartheid regime. Governments imposed economic sanctions, and the United Nations provided political and economic support to the African National Congress. Intergovernmental organizations dispatched groups of eminent statesmen to mediate. Churches mobilized the public conscience, and university students carried out protests. Under intense pressure, corporations made decisions to stop investing in South Africa.

Even more critical were inside Third Siders. While Nelson Mandela and F. W. de Klerk were solidly rooted in their own groups, fighting hard to protect their interests, they also played the curious role of Third Siders, seeking a nonviolent resolution.

Working with them were thousands of other insiders determined to reach across the chasm of color. Church and business leaders came together with the white government, the African National Congress, and other political groups to devise the National Peace Accord, an unprecedented countrywide network of dispute resolution committees at the local, regional, and national levels. The committees, made up of people from the different communities who had never talked or worked with each other before, succeeded in defusing a great many violent confrontations between white police and black citizens and provided a training ground in grassroots democracy. Thus emerged a critical mass of inside Third Siders, a strong new center capable of withstanding the polarizing pressure of the extremists on each side.

The surprising magnitude and speed of transformation in South Africa cannot be explained by a change of mind alone; a change in heart and spirit were required. Imprisoned for 27 years, treated harshly by whites, Nelson Mandela somehow found it within himself to forgive his white captors, the oppressors of his race. When I heard him speak about his white adversaries, I was impressed that his voice and demeanor betrayed no rancor. And while this inner change of heart was the solitary soul-searching act of an individual, it did not stop there. For, in the hope of reconstructing a South Africa in which blacks and whites could live together in peace and prosperity, Mandela succeeded in persuading first his colleagues and then his people to tread the same difficult path of forgiveness and reconciliation. An individual act of spirit thereby became an emotional shift among millions, a political force with far-reaching effects.

Because it is not as tangible as an outsider or an insider, the "inner Third Side" is harder to describe. However nebulous, its power cannot be denied because, in the final analysis, deep-seeded conflict is resolved largely through the emotional, psychological, and spiritual work of the parties. The Third Side manifests itself as a kind of conscience within the single individual engaged in conflict. It is the voice that urges us to heal old grievances, the capacity to listen to the other side and show empathy, the impulse to respect the basic human needs of all. The inner Third Side instinctively values life and abhors violence.

Outsiders empower insiders, insiders mobilize outsiders, and both are inspired by an inner Third Side. Working together, they can transform even an intractable conflict such as South Africa.

The Third Side, in short, is *people* from the community; using a certain kind of *power,* the power of peers; from a certain *perspective,* of common ground; supporting a certain *process,* of dialogue and nonviolence; and aiming for a certain *product,* a "triple win" – a resolution that satisfies the legitimate needs of the parties *and* at the same time meets the needs of the wider community.

The Third Side is the emergent will of the community. It is an impulse that arises from the vital relationships linking each member and every other member of the community. People can contribute to the Third Side, but no one commands it. It is *self-organizing* with its own natural laws.

A serviceable analogy for the Third Side is the body's immune system. When a cell is attacked by a virus, it sends out a chemical alarm awakening the dendritic cells that lie dormant in every tissue of the body. The dendritic cells, in turn, mobilize the T-cells, which come to the rescue. If the T-cells roughly correspond to the police and peacekeepers of the world, the dendritic cells correspond to the surrounding community that must be aroused in order to stop destructive conflict. The Third Side thus serves as a kind of *social immune system* preventing the spread of the virus of violence.

Peace is Possible, If . . .

To the question of whether we can transform even serious conflicts into creative conflict and cooperation, the answer is "Yes, *if.*" Yes, if we seize the opportunity before us. Yes, if we assume the *responsibility* of becoming Third Siders. Yes, if we do the hard work. The "if," in each of these aspects, depends on us.

The "if" is not a little "if"; it is a big "IF." In dealing with our own conflicts, it is not easy to face the pain of human differences. It takes more courage to look in the mirror to find fault than to gaze into the telescope to do so. It takes courage to forgive and apologize. It requires patience to listen and search for agreement.

Intervening in other people's conflicts can be equally hard. No one likes to be accused of meddling. No one wants to risk straining relationships with friends, relatives, and allies. It is frightening to get involved in a potentially volatile or actually violent situation. Taking the Third Side is no easy task.

In the sheer magnitude and complexity of the challenge, the struggle for peace, ironically enough, most closely resembles nothing so much as war itself. Think of how much work goes into preparing for and engaging in wars. No less effort is required for the sake of peace. Think too about the virtues required of warriors. Courage? Peace demands just as much; facing up to force nonviolently calls for perhaps even more bravery and self-control than fighting. Cooperation and discipline? Solidarity and altruism? All these ingredients are needed to transform treacherous conflicts. The peace we can aspire to, then, is not a harmonious peace of the grave, nor a submissive peace of the slave, but a hard-working peace of the brave.

If we prove successful as Third Siders, as I believe we will, schoolchildren may wonder one day why serious conflicts ever escalated to terrible violence and war. They may be astonished why we did not take the simple precautions necessary to prevent a conflagration. They may puzzle over why people did not see that, whatever an effective prevention system might cost in time and effort, its price is but a pittance compared to the exorbitant cost of destructive conflict. They may wonder why we took so long to make what will seem to them an obvious choice.

As the Ethiopian proverb goes, "When spider webs unite, they can halt even a lion." Each Third Side step we take for peace is like a single spider web. Alone, it cannot do much perhaps, but together with many other steps, it can accomplish the task. The hope of humanity lies in weaving a series of spider webs strong enough to halt the lion of violence and war.

28

Risking Hospitality

Martin Marty

The roots of human aggression are deep and in many ways mysterious. In the eyes of some evolutionary biologists, humans may be descended from a particular violent simian strain. To some schools of sociology, they are territorial aggressors, naturally protecting space or acquiring it in order to survive. Their activities often are murderous, since some other animals are doing the same to their space. In many mythical traditions humans fight humans because they are acting out a primordial story that is based in violence. Most religions have their own accounting for these aspects of human life. Thus the majority of Christians have their version of the Genesis story of "the Fall" and deduce doctrines – for some, original sin – that pit them against others, who have equal propensities for violence and evil.

On the other hand, the human record is also rich with stories of human concord. People may know that they appear to be naturally violent, but through a variety of philosophies they find value in being peaceful. Through generous and self-sacrificial activities they care for others, both as individuals and in groups, as peoples. In some cultures they draft concordats or constitutions which help assure that there are other than violent means for addressing human needs and for serving the common good. In some myths and religious stories there are what Abraham Lincoln called "better angels of our nature," and both in observation and in doctrine they come to declare that humans have benign instincts.

Religion: it happens that, to use gamblers' terms, it "raises the stakes" on both sides of human nature, action, and story. Religion is the healer that kills, the killer that heals. More precisely, religions don't kill or heal: people who carry their messages, believe their claims, accept their promises, and act on what they regard to be their commands, are the healers and killers. Sometimes the religious impulses and actions contradict each other: a military leader may feel called to kill enemies and see his own people killed – and yet also be known as someone who is tender with children, who visits and consoles captured enemies, and the like.

What is it about religion that it can do both of these, can exist at the extremes of human conduct, can impel people to outrageously destructive and admirably constructive ends? Religion, the scholars tell us, begins in awe: awe before "the Other," God or Force or Energy or Connection or Idea. In any case, the confrontation with the Other is experienced as an overload. People who have a religious experience characteristically seek or form company, for support or to promote more powerful, because common, activity. There they receive mandates and missions: "Free the people!" "Kill the loathsome races that profane God!"

The messages and intentions of different sets of people – whether following racial, tribal, national, or common interest lines – will clash with others who promote or follow theirs. In our time, around the world people gather compulsively into angry masses and direct their actions against others, who are doing the same. But different sets of people can also be brought to see the futility of their lethal conflict. Doing so is never easy, and can be almost impossible to pursue after conflict has begun. So preventive and smaller-scale actions are often the place to start.

How can "the better angels of our nature" be made to show up in actions that religion justifies? The notion that clashes among civilizations, cultures, societies, and nations would end if religion were *abolished* is not borne out by history. The zealot leaders of the great "-isms" of the century just past – fascism, communism, Nazism, and Maoism, just for beginnings – wanted to replace or suppress religion. They were unsuccessful, after decades of bloodbathing at the expense of millions of lives. (They often took on some of the characteristics of religions themselves, with myths and symbols, rites and ceremonies, prescriptions and practices.) None of them provided any promise of concord other than through the subjugation of everyone else in their realm, or the world, to their iron control.

At the opposite extreme, some advocate a solution based on the dream of developing a *single religion*, one that is inclusive, synthetic, and benign. Their utopian scenarios strike most people as being dystopian: in a winner-take-all approach to synthesis and merger, someone (most people!) would be left out. The human story is far too rich, its people too diverse, their interests too varied, for them to agree voluntarily on the deepest things in their lives. Efforts to invent inclusive religions usually lead to fission among merging parties. Where there had been two to unite, now there are three: the uniters and the two groups "back home" who broke off from them.

These two "no-religion" and "one-religion" approaches are not on the horizon, and would not be welcomed by most people if they were pressed. So only a third choice is available as an alternative to conflict among the religions. They must somehow come into conversation.

Conversation is not the same as argument. *Argument* is guided by the answers, not the questions. If you have the answers about the divine, the sacred, the mysteries, God, and power, you either have to convert me, humiliate me, exile me, or kill me. Conversation is guided by the questions, not the answers. Each of us, as individuals and as parties, can bring our commitments, and learn to respect those of others.

Where the two parties (nations, religions, churches, interests, ethnic groups, etc.) can be brought to meet, they are free to search for and may well find much that they have in common. They will treat their differences in different ways. In common, we can speak with some hope of this because as the last century went on great numbers of ecumenical, interfaith, and interreligious conversations were begun, and they prosper. Often they look modest, or are overlooked, because they are so homely, so domestic, so localized. People of different nations, races, and religions have often expressed common devotion to human rights, human dignity, some version or other of the "sacredness" of people.

Once assured that they enter into conversation with their rights and dignity protected, they are free to display their particularities. That is, "down deep," religions live not by least common denominators, the surface beliefs, the broad tenets, the vague patterns of conduct that are easy to reach with others. They live what philosopher George Santayana called the surprising and often idiosyncratic stories they tell. These are the motivators of action; they engender salvific activities and provoke responses. They are not all in conflict with the stories others tell; there are congruences, points of overlap, surprising agreements that come out of true meetings. People who have reached such levels of empathy are not likely to be instigators or supporters of war.

Still, the stories and beliefs, the customs and practices, of the various companies of people (which can mean their religions, their ethnic groups, their "caste" among social classes) will differ significantly. What to do?

First, say many: turn *tolerant*. The discovery and promotion of tolerance was a great boon in early modern times in the West, and it has parallels in Eastern and Southern worlds as well. However, in today's culture, tolerance can come cheap and easy: "If I can get you to believe as little as I do, and to hold to it as lightly as I do, things will work out." That is unsatisfying, especially when or because the other group may not want to believe little and hold it lightly.

One step up, and this I borrow from Gabriel Marcel, is the concept of *counter-intolerance*. That is the expression of people who believe something so deeply and are situated in a community or communion so well that they are tempted to be intolerant of those in other communities who hold different ideas. One is tempted to be intolerant. Yet it is possible to be schooled to approach the situation in a different way. I use the depth of my own commitment and the bonding of my own community as a warrant to the other: I understand how hard it is to find meaning in life, and to pursue it in company. I will use my understanding to help assure you that yours and your interests are guaranteed.

Let me carry it one step further, to what I call *risking hospitality*. Most of the religions have some notion of hospitality. One must take in the stranger, even in nomadic societies without bank vaults or walls. Of course, we are wise enough today to keep our fingers crossed, to be suspicious and alert. But using our heads is not the last strategy. Eyes wide open, one still hosts.

Start on the domestic level, which can be both practical and metaphoric for the larger scene.

Come to my home, you Jew or Hindu or Muslim, enjoy my table, but do not expect me to remove the Christian cross, without which my home would be incomplete and, in my view, spiritually impoverished. Yet I will speak differently and learn more carefully because you are here, since I want to learn who you are and find some measure of communion. You, a Jew, invited me to your home on a Friday night: I do not expect or want you to skip the Shabbat rituals. I have accepted your invitation in order to learn to know more about you, your life, life as mediated through your faith. You will listen and speak differently, as will I, and we will both have grown in our relation and our place in the world.

Of course, working that out on a world scale is more difficult, the processes more cumbersome, the yield more uncertain. You are *risking* hospitality, not assuring this or that outcome. But a review of the good moments and movements of the last century, a review that will lift out some proper names – Mohandas Gandhi, Pope John XXIII, Martin Luther King, Jr, Dorothy Day, Nelson Mandela, and thousands more – will show that moments of breakthrough come in the mix of tolerance, counter-intolerance, and risked hospitality that go with conversation by individuals or groups. They know there is no alternative that holds promise – only the threat of hateful and vengeful acts, and the terrors of war. Religious people may be "warriors for God" in some circumstances. The final vision of most of their sacred books are promises of peace, which they are to pursue.

Index